0075 Chair at Do.
R. Ta

2-25

Along the Way

by

James J. Tarr

*I have taught thee in the way of wisdom; I have led
thee in right paths.*
Proverbs 4:11

authorHOUSE™

1663 LIBERTY DRIVE, SUITE 200
BLOOMINGTON, INDIANA 47403
(800) 839-8640
WWW.AUTHORHOUSE.COM

First published by AuthorHouse 08/10/04

ISBN: 1-4184-8430-X (sc)

Library of Congress Control Number: 2004095249

Printed in the United States of America
Bloomington, Indiana
This book is printed on acid-free paper.

All Scripture is quoted from the Authorized King James Version.

Table of Contents

Dedicated

to my three sons, Bill, Dan, and Jim

for faithfully supporting me and their mother

during these many years

In Appreciation

I wish to express sincere thanks to the many who have helped make my dream a reality. From the very beginning when I felt a burden from the Lord to put down on paper the lessons I have learned in my life, God has provided the right people at the right time to encourage and direct me. I want to thank Barbara Sleicher and Heidi Bond for typing many pages and deciphering my handwriting. Also, I would like to express my gratitude to Catherine Anthony for her fine work of editing. Lastly, thanks to George Dollar and Elaine Johnson for their help.

Preface

My experiences have not been unique. Over the years I have watched others walk a similar path. Solomon wrote in Ecclesiastes 1:9, *"The thing that hath been, it is that which shall be; and that which is done is that which shall be done: and there is no new thing under the sun."* So why repeat what others have said or written? I can only say that it is because I have felt prompted by the Holy Spirit to record these thoughts. So whatever may be the outcome of this endeavor is not under my control, obedience is.

Sometimes the Holy Spirit uses a thought from a verse of Scripture as a directive for life. Thusly, the words of Isaiah 24:15 took on special meaning to me: *"Wherefore glorify ye the Lord in the fires, even the name of the LORD GOD of Israel in the isles of the sea."* The experiences of my life have had a purpose, even when they were not particularly pleasant, and that was to glorify the Lord. I have sought to relate some of the ways that the Lord has worked in my life down through the years, trusting that ultimately they will bring glory to His Name... *"O God Thou hast taught me from my youth: and hitherto have I declared Thy wondrous works. Now also when I am old and grey headed, O God, forsake me not; until I have showed Thy strength unto this generation, and Thy power to everyone that is to come."* Psalm 71:17, 18.

Introduction

How do you read this book? What a strange question! Yet, is it not the attitude of your mind and heart that help you benefit from what you read? You may find that you can relate to some of the events in this book while others may be out of the realm of your experience. However, please don't read any lightly.

Over the years I have been impressed by words of advice that the Lord later used to enlighten my path. In my reading or listening the Holy Spirit has italicized in my mind ideas He wanted recorded in my memory.

Then at the right time He bas brought them to mind to teach me and help me to choose the right path.

For me there has never been an audible voice as was heard by Moses or the Apostle Paul. There has never been an experience comparable to that of Isaiah. My direction has come one step at a time. For me to get from A to C to fulfill the will of God there was always a B. Over and over the Lord has taught me that today's experiences are preparation for tomorrow's service. Fulfilling the will of God is usually not one dramatic step, but many little ones taken over a period of time.

The fact is no one at birth has all the qualifications and ability to be proficient in anything. A doctor is not born with a brain already programmed, eliminating the need for formal education. The skills he possesses today have been acquired, and his learning never ends. So is it in the life of a Christian. At the time of his spiritual birth he embarks upon a spiritual education. Each new experience helps to conform the Christian to the image of Jesus Christ, while at the same time equipping him for service. As one grows in the Christian life, he will be able to say to a struggling babe in Christ, "I've been there; I know what it is like. This is what the Lord taught me *along the way.*"

Childhood Memories

A Christian Heritage

As I look back from this vantage point of age, I realize that the greatest privilege I had was to be reared in a Christian atmosphere. At the time I felt my parents were too strict for not permitting me to do, say, or go as I pleased. Though next to the youngest in the family, we all followed the same basic rules. Talking back to my parents was never permitted. Four-letter words were forbidden. If we talked back, sassed, or used a four-letter word, the penalty was black pepper sprinkled on the tongue, and black pepper had its own unique way of teaching one to guard his language (I suppose today such parental action would be called "child abuse").

No, my parents weren't mean and unreasonable. They sensed their responsibility to *"train us in the way we ought to go"* (Proverbs 22:6) and their accountability to God as parents to *"bring us up in the fear and admonition of the Lord"* (Ephesians 6:4). Their main desire was for each of us to accept Jesus Christ as Savior (John 3:3) and avoid the pitfalls of the devil. To them our eternal destiny was more important than all the luxuries they might provide.

Going to church Sunday morning and evening was routine in all seasons, and in order that we might be on time for Sunday School, most of us got a bath Saturday afternoon or evening. Walking a mile and a half or so to church was never considered to be too far, and remaining for the Worship Service was considered important for our spiritual growth.

Walking home was always fun. Each of us took turns closing our eyes, while the others led the victim into a tree or off the curb without warning. And since we were very young and gullible, we believed that we would "break our mother's back "if we stepped on a crack.

Sunday dinner was the biggest meal of the week. During the meal, we were allowed to talk for or against any subject except the preacher. If one of us would make a comment about the pastor, our dad would sternly say, "We are not going to have 'Roast Preacher' for dinner." He was teaching us the Biblical principle of respecting the one called of God to shepherd the flock.

No doubt each of us can recall some special childhood experience. My first special memory happened in first grade. I fell in love. My first grade teacher had me spell-bound. She had dark hair and a beautiful smile. Sitting in my seat, I dreamed of the day when I would catch up to her age and ask her to marry me. But then it happened. One day the principal of the school opened our classroom door and asked to speak with my teacher in the hall. The last thing she said to us was to be quiet while she was out of the room talking with the principal. As soon as the door closed behind her, erasers and paper-wads began to fly back and forth. The noise got so loud she opened the door just long enough to warn us to "be quiet or else."

When she finally returned to the classroom, she asked who was making all the racket. Because no one spoke, she instructed all of us to stand and get in line. Then, one by one, each took his turn in the cloak-room for a spanking. I and a few others did not participate in the ruckus but sat quietly at our desk like she asked us to do. Though I told her that I had not joined in with the noisemakers, she spanked me anyway. It was at that moment I cancelled my future wedding plans. I wasn't going to marry any woman with whom I couldn't reason. (Pretty smart for a six-year-old, wouldn't you say!)

A second recollection was of a more serious nature. It was one of those rare moments when I had my mother all to myself. With five others vying for her time, such a luxury didn't happen often. I think I already knew the answer to the question I was about to ask, but I wanted it verified: "Mother, do you love me more than the others; am I your favorite child?" Very gently she took me by the arm and said, "Jimmy, I want you to sit down beside me." Pulling me close to her, she went on to say, "In my heart there is a place reserved for each of you. There is a place reserved just for you. Your brothers and sisters cannot enter your area nor can you enter theirs. In my heart you are very special, and the special I feel for you I feel equally for the others. You cannot take one another's place."

Her answer did not disappoint me, for though I was young, I really didn't want it any other way. Now that I am older, her answer has helped me to understand more clearly the very heart of God. In His heart there is a very special place for me, and though we be many, He loves each of His children equally. He is not influenced by our ethnic background, academic achievement or color of skin. He has no favorites.

Sickness

Chest colds in late fall and winter was as predictable as the coming snow, but one chest cold would be different. The rubbing of Vicks or a dry mustard plaster on the chest, which had helped on previous occasions, was ineffective, and fearing that I might have pneumonia, the family doctor was summoned.

When the doctor arrived, I was struggling for oxygen and my lips were blue. Immediately he opened his satchel and gave me medicine. Within half-an-hour the frightful struggle to breathe had eased and normal color had returned to my lips. The diagnosis? "Bronchial asthma." This would be the first episode with many more to follow. In fact, it became a chronic condition.

A year or so later the doctor noticed that I had not grown even a quarter of an inch or gained one pound, so he prescribed a T.B. test along with x-rays of the chest and lungs. The T.B. test proved negative, but the x-rays revealed that my bronchial tubes were severely damaged by prolonged, heavy coughing. The doctor advised my parents to move to Arizona for the sake of my health. Though they wanted to do all they could for the sake of my health, it was financially impossible

to move. Therefore, the next option was to get a shot

in the arm two or three times a week during the cold,

blustery months to fortify the immune system. Though

I never looked forward to the shots, they did seem to

lessen the frequency and severity of the attacks.

Moving On Up

High School

After eight years of schooling, I received a diploma, but it wasn't the diploma in hand that excited me most. It was the fact that I could proudly claim a new title: "Freshman in High School." For some reason the title made me feel older and smarter. Supposedly I could now speak with authority. I could even challenge my parents' advice.

Like most freshman, I was anxious on the first day of class. Would I say or do something dumb that would give away my new status? Dare I ask another student for directions (another tell-tale sign)? And though I was smiling on the outside, could others detect my stomach was churning?

Though these questions were big issues, a larger one loomed inside. How did I want to portray myself to my fellow classmates? How did I want them to think of me? This was an important decision because years earlier I had accepted Jesus Christ as my personal Savior. Was I going to let the entire student body know that I was a "born again" Christian or would they see me as a boy who would not swear or tell dirty stories? To my regret, I chose the latter. But why? Shamefully I confess two reasons. First, I wanted to be popular and be elected class president. The second reason was pride. At the time I was not willing to bear the marks of a Christian. Even to this day I can't sing the hymn "At Calvary" without feeling the words deeply. Oh, I did care that He was crucified for me, but "years I spent in vanity and **pride**" described me exactly for it was my pride that kept me from living openly for Christ. As it turned out, the students I was afraid to tell about Christ because they were popular were led to the Lord later in life. I lost the opportunity to be the one to tell them and receive Christ's blessing.

As to my behavior during high school days, I wasn't getting drunk, nor was I guilty of so-called "baser" sins. I was, however, guilty of going places and doing things that I knew displeased the Lord. Perhaps smiling and laughing outwardly, I would be praying inwardly, "Lord, please don't come just now. I don't want to be in this place when you come." Now I can't tell you the many times I went through the same routine, but one night I experienced an event that had a greater impact on my walk with the Lord than any sermon I had ever heard.

Where I was and with whom that evening is now irrelevant. It was what I saw when I returned to our two-story home. It was late and I was tired, so I decided to go right up to bed. As I walked down the lighted hallway, the door to my parents' bedroom was slightly ajar. Looking in so that I might say good-night, I saw my mother, enveloped by the hallway light, kneeling in prayer at her bedside. The sight brought deep conviction to my soul, for I knew my behavior had disappointed the Lord that evening. She too would have been disappointed had she known what the Lord knew. As I knelt in prayer that night, I asked the Lord to help me to be a Christ-like Christian, a stepping stone, and not a stumbling block. The sad note is that I never told her how the sight of her kneeling in prayer had influenced my walk with the Lord.

Decisions, decisions. Such was the challenge of my freshman year. The male students no longer had to be nagged by their mothers to comb their hair, brush their teeth, or change their socks, for now there were many silent voices to say all these and more, namely, *girls*.

After my concern for my personal appearance was my choice of curriculum: Academic, Commercial or General, sports or joining a club that had specific goals. After making these choices in the first few weeks of school, I had to resolve another question: whom would I ask for that first date? How should I approach a girl to ask her? "Hey, you?" What would I say? What does a boy do if his voice cracks when asking a girl? If she says she already has a date, is she telling the truth, or is it a polite way of saying "No"?

By trial and error I overcame my timidity by my junior year. After taking different girls to different school activities, many of my classmates became attracted to one girl, and they were seen at all social activities with the same date, "going steady."

Though I had my drivers license when a junior, I did not have my own car. So in order to use the family car, I had to abide by two requirements: 1, I had to be home with the car no later than 11 p.m., and 2, I would have to take the girl to church if I was going to drive the car Sunday evening.

The arrangement was perfect. Most school activities were on Friday night, and the girl I wanted to be "steady" with lived in a rural area, so I needed a car. She wanted to go steady too, so she was happy to hear that there would now be a way for us to be together. The stipulation about going to church Sunday evenings did not create a problem, for the church she attended regularly on Sunday morning did not have an evening church service.

While I was caught up with dating and school activities, there was a dark cloud hanging over America. Every American's life was affected by the ongoing Second World War. Most students had either a family member, relative, neighbor, or friend serving in the Armed Forces. Before we started our senior year, however, a peace treaty was signed with Germany and Japan. Servicemen were coming home from active duty, but the call for recruits was still being heard from all the branches of military service. New men were needed to fill the gap left by those who had fought so long and hard.

With patriotism still running high, many young men in my class wanted to serve our country and they planned to enlist in one of the branches of the military immediately after graduation. I was one of them. Naturally every relationship was affected. The night before boarding a Greyhound bus with classmates to travel to Pittsburgh, Pennsylvania, to enlist, my girlfriend and I talked a long time about our relationship while I was away. We agreed that it would be acceptable for either of us to date other people. Though I had dated other girls before she and I began to date, I was the first and only boy she had ever dated. And so we said goodbye.

Arriving at the Pittsburgh induction center five days after graduation, we new high school graduates were quickly introduced to "Hurry up and wait." All went well for me until the doctor asked the question, "Do you have asthma?" Though I knew what he meant, I said, "No," for I didn't have the symptoms at the moment the question was asked. I reasoned that if they didn't take me that day as an enlistee, I would probably be drafted a few months later when the qualifications would be eased. In fact, the one and only classmate who failed the physical that day was later accepted.

Engagement and Break Up

I was assigned by the army to report to Camp Lee, Virginia, for Basic Training. Then, when I completed the course, it was on to Ft. Oglethorpe, Georgia, to complete a Postal course. From there I returned to Camp Lee to wait for further assignment.

By then, warm summer days had ended, and cold, blustery, rainy days had returned, the very weather that always led to one of my bronchial asthma attacks. And so it happened. For the next few weeks, depending on the weather, I was in and out of the army hospital. As long as the weather was good, I had no problems, but as soon as the weather changed to cold and rainy, I had another attack. Finally, I confessed to the doctor about my battle with chronic bronchial asthma since childhood and was given an "Honorable Medical Discharge."

When I returned home, I got a job at the Hazel Atlas Glass Factory. Finally, a regular income, so I could purchase a used car. I was still dating the same girl and attending the Sunday evening church service as usual. We were enjoying a good relationship, so the next step was a diamond ring. Naturally our plans were serious, and eventually we got around to the subject of our spiritual lives.

I had assumed that because she had never mentioned responding to an altar call at the end of the message on Sunday evening, she understood that those who did so were accepting Jesus Christ as Savior, acknowledging that they had sinned and needed to be "born again." Unfortunately, her personal belief was based on what she had heard her own pastor say: "A God of love would never send anybody to Hell." (Actually, God has done all He needs to do to keep people out of Hell. He has made a way of escape – faith in Jesus

Christ). Accepting the idea that her pastor had taught, she concluded that everybody would go to Heaven, but that if someone felt better by publicly accepting Christ that was okay but not necessary to get to Heaven.

Sorry to say, there are many who have the same mistaken idea. Years later, when endeavoring to lead a young lady to Christ, I got a similar response. As a little girl she had asked her pastor what to do in order to go to Heaven. His response was, "Do the best that you can in life. That is all that God expects." Now if that be so, Calvary's cross was a cruel act of God. If John 3:16 is not true, how can anyone believe any part of the Bible? In fact, no person can rightly believe there is a Heaven for believers' everlasting life if he does not accept the fact that there is a Hell where those who do not believe or trust in Jesus Christ will perish.

The primary source of our knowledge of the existence of Heaven is Divine Revelation. The thought of its existence did not originate with man. Therefore, to believe in Heaven, one must believe in Divine Revelation. It is also true that the knowledge of the existence of Hell is by Divine Revelation. Now, if one does not accept the revelation of the existence of Hell for the unbeliever, he has no right to believe in the existence of Heaven for the believer, for each knowledge comes from the same source.

My reaction to my fiancé's acceptance of her pastor's statement was surprise and concern. How would this difference of belief affect our future life together? I knew I would want to go to church Sunday morning, evening and Wednesday night, but would she? What if we were blessed with children? Would she pray for their salvation as I would? More importantly, how could I disobey 2 Corinthians 6:14? At the time, the only solution that I could see was to lay aside the whole issue and pray that she would accept

Christ as her Savior, which would clear the way for our marriage.

In the meantime, the Lord was dealing with me. Every Sunday evening for a number of weeks the Holy Spirit led my pastor to say Matthew 6:33: "But seek ye first the kingdom of God and His righteousness, and all these things shall be added unto you." During the week, the Lord did not allow me to forget these words.

On the fifth or sixth Sunday evening, the thrust of his message was the necessity for the child of God to put Christ first before all people, all things, for all time. With the Holy Spirit tugging at my heart when the altar call was given, I began to step into the center aisle. As I did, I felt a tug on the sleeve of my sports coat. I turned to my fiancé and asked if she wanted to go forward with me. Perhaps my prayer for her salvation would now be answered. Her answer was "No." I asked,

"Why did you pull on my sleeve?" She answered, "I don't want you to go." In that second I knew I had to make a decision, one that would affect my entire future. Would I remain in my seat with this girl to whom I was engaged or would I go forward to publicly proclaim my desire to obey God? I left her standing there and walked down a long aisle alone where I knelt at the altar and yielded my life to Jesus Christ.

On the way home from church we said nothing about my commitment to Christ, but slowly in the ensuing months, our paths began to separate. Then one evening she said, "I've tried your way for a long time, now I want you to try mine." I knew I could not change course, yet, even though I knew what was coming, I denied the possibility of an inevitable break in our relationship. Reality soon caught up to me, however, when she returned my ring, breaking our engagement. I refused to take the ring. "It will never do me any good."

The months to follow were difficult for me, but now in hindsight I realize I created my own sorrow. I have learned that it is possible to be so involved emotionally that I make decisions from my heart instead of my head. My head may say one thing, while my heart overrules all known Biblical instructions. The Biblical instruction of 2 Corinthians 6:14 is "Be ye not unequally yoked together with unbelievers." Those words do not imply that believers are better than unbelievers, but that there is a different set of values for believers than for unbelievers. That is what she meant when she said, "I tried your way for a while, now you try mine." Should she be living today I would thank her for her courage to end our relationship. She could foresee what I refused to acknowledge: "Can two walk together except they be agreed?" (Amos 3:3). I have devised the following analogy. You may tie a dog and a cat together by the tail and create unity (marriage), but I dare say you will not have created harmony. Each one will pull in the opposite direction. Happy marriages are created by two like-minded people pulling in the same direction – God-ward. In a book written for teenagers a Christian author wrote that for a Christian to be going steady with an unbeliever is like getting all dressed up with no place to go.

Like all wounds, they can and do heal. And eventually I began to date again.

All the Light in One Place

At last I had come out of hiding and openly let it be known that I was a born-again Christian. I experienced great relief. I would not turn back. Though many close friends knew of my spiritual experience my challenge was to be a witness to my fringe acquaintances and co-workers. To have the opportunity to witness to the men with whom I worked without interfering with their responsibilities would take two years. I had no set plan, but each day made myself available to the Lord to speak through me.

The department in which I worked was called "The Hot End," because it was the hot end of a glass factory containing hot molten glass.

My first title on the job was "Sweeper," a descriptive title for a job that entailed sweeping up broken glass that had fallen on the floor so that the feet and ankles of the workers would not be cut. My first promotion was to "Spare Operator," which was an apprentice position for the full operation of one of the machines. But while observing and learning the functions of the machine, the Spare Operator was also to give two ten-minute breaks per shift to each operator. I used my breaks to visit another department in the plant and talk with an older man who also was a Christian. Talking with him about the things of the Lord was always a time of learning and encouragement, so encouraging that I said to him, "Wouldn't it be good if I worked here with you in this department and we could talk more often about the things of the Lord?" Surprisingly, he said that it was not a good idea. I asked, "Why not?" He answered, "My light is needed here in my department and your light is needed in your department. If we worked together, we would have all the light in one place."

Though the words were spoken in broken English, they were used by the Lord to lead me to the next step He was directing me to take. At the time I was very much involved in the things of the Lord with others of my age in the church. However, the Holy Spirit kept reminding me of the thought, "All the light in one place." No other statement was as significant in shaping my decision to prepare for the ministry. We Christians possess the light while millions sit in darkness.

Education

Now it didn't take long for the news to spread that I was planning to go to college to prepare for the ministry. News spread rapidly in my hometown. In fact, when I sat in my dentist chair he inquired about my plans (He too had heard). Then to my surprise he stated that he had talked it over with one of his colleagues about helping me financially to go to college. The two would pay for my tuition, books, room and board and other related expenses. However, the offer to help financially was not to be extended for studies at the college of my choice but one of theirs. The one he named was very prestigious, but its theology program was said to be liberal. He did not expect an answer that afternoon but he urged me to make a decision as soon as possible for it was already late to submit an application for admittance.

This offer was certainly enticing but other factors had to be taken into consideration. For instance, I had already sent a late application to the school of my choice and was waiting for a reply.

My battle with chronic bronchial asthma as a little boy had ended with an honorable medical discharge from the army, and even though I had been unable to complete the total time for which I had enlisted, enough active duty days were served to entitle me to two years of college. The choice now was an education with all expenses paid in a college where the whole Bible was not regarded as Truth or a college where God's Word was wholly taught but where I would have to trust the Lord for funds to complete my education. I chose the later for in no way could I ever, as a future pastor, deny the fundamentals of the faith.

Work Place

When planning to make a major move, many begin a countdown. So it was with me. I had worked two years at the same job with the same group of men, and then with an acceptance letter from the Missionary Training Institute (now Nyack College), I submitted two weeks notice to my employer that I was leaving for college. In one sense, I had completed a mission, for during those two years of work, I had talked quietly with each man at work concerning his need to accept Jesus Christ as his personal Savior. All but one had listened intently.

Now I should point out that the men with whom I worked behaved each day like most unsaved men. It seemed that each one wanted his behavior to show that he was not a religious person. Immoral remarks were a way of life, and knowing that I would not participate in a vulgar conversation, I had been "set up" on many occasions. It worked like this! While I was in serious conversation with a fellow worker, two or three others would get together to decide which one of them would begin to tell a smutty joke to us knowing that I would leave quickly. Then, especially for my hearing the fellow would spew out foul language. Though this action was annoying, I had to remind myself that Christ had died for each of these men.

My last half hour of working with these older men was spent saying good-bye. I started at one end of the department and said a word to each one. About half-way through the department, I came to one man who lowered his head and shuffled his feet. "Jim, I owe you an apology," he said. "When I learned that you were a Christian, I tried the best way I knew to break you, but I couldn't. You have proven to me that you are real, and I know that whatever you do in life will be successful."

His words flew right by me, but I shuttered at his words, "I tried to break you." What if he had succeeded? What would have been his reaction if I had listened to any one of those dirty stories? Sometimes it is easy to forget that we are surrounded by spiritual darkness and that God has placed us where we are. We may grumble about the job God has provided for our daily livelihood.

As a little boy I remember waiting for the arrival of one of God's creations. The gardens had been planted and the days and nights were warm enough. I wanted to be the first to announce to all who cared," I just saw a lightening bug!" Soon little blinkers, like Christmas lights, would be seen in every neighborhood. Running in the yard with a pint jar in one hand and a vented lid in the other, we would attempt to snatch a firefly in flight before its light went out. Part of the fun was guessing the direction of its flight when its light was in the off mode.

Then, with a jar half full of lightening bugs, what did we do with them? On each finger of each hand there would be a glowing ring, like a king or queen would wear. The bugs that survived this ordeal were placed under the bed as a one night "night light."

As the nights became cooler, sightings were less often. Then finally the evening came. Peering into the darkness, we would wait and wait. At last one little lamp could be seen. In reality, it would not be brighter than those we had seen before but because it was the only one in the darkness of night, it appeared much brighter than it was. This is true of the Christian's light when he finds himself in a workplace of spiritual darkness. Perhaps then he remembers one of the first songs he learned as a toddler and knows its true meaning – "This little light of mine. I'm gonna let it shine!"

MTI

Healing

College life was a whirlwind. The car needed to be sold, for without a regular income, I could no longer afford to keep it. Shopping for clothing and suitcases, arranging for transportation to campus, all had to be done. Sharing my testimony with the church family in the last Sunday evening service before leaving was high on my list of things to do. There did not seem to be enough time for it all, but it was all accomplished.

Arriving at the campus, I felt like I needed a week's vacation. The first few days I completed registration, orientation, choosing courses and learning the location of buildings and classrooms. We were all given a copy of the school's calendar. The first date I looked for was the last day of the school year, and then I checked to see when the first class break was scheduled. It would not be until Thanksgiving, but another fall event was listed: "Spiritual Emphasis Week." Though I did not understand the meaning of this event, the upperclassmen knew a guest speaker would minister to the student body every evening and during an extended chapel period in the morning of the week.

When that week arrived, the students entered the chapel with great anticipation. They had been praying for spiritual blessing, and for me the week would be a major step in my Christian life. I had already surrendered my life to the Lord in my home church, but there remained two questions about my surrender: 1, how deeply sincere was my surrender? and 2, how long would it last?

After his opening remarks, our guest speaker announced the theme of his messages: "I Believe God." In that first message and those to follow in the next two days, my heart was blessed. But at the same time, I had something gnawing in my soul.

Until this time, my experience was similar to testimonies from other Christians. I too would sing, "I'll go where you want me to go, dear Lord...Fully surrendered, Lord I would be...Where He leads me I will follow," while in my heart I would be saying, "Lord, I'll be anything but a missionary." That was the silent message and attitude of my heart which only the Lord knew. The words "I Believe God" would play a major role in my life in the next few days.

As it happened, the illness that had followed me since childhood and the reason for my medical discharge from military service was active again. Though it was not severe, one evening, I was wheezing, a reminder of things past and possibly of things to come.

Listening to a message, I heard the speaker challenge the student body to believe God for any and every need. He gave an invitation to come forward to the altar to pray and believe God to meet our needs. I responded to the call. My need – that God would heal me of bronchial asthma. For if I would be able to go out in all types of weather to minister as a Pastor, I would need to be healed of this malady.

As I knelt at the altar, I said, "Lord, I'll even be a missionary." I was foolish, for I was not indispensable to God for His work. I was not doing God a favor by surrendering. I would be the beneficiary. I have learned that the one who yields himself to the Lord always receives His gifts. The marvel is not that I surrendered, but that He would be willing to trust me with proclaiming the gospel message.

Now my yielding was not a trade-off: "If you heal me then I'll be a missionary." No, this was a more complete surrender. As the preacher anointed and prayed for me, the Lord healed me instantly. I got up from that altar, and from that moment I have been in all types of weather for over fifty years without one bronchial asthma attack. I have had colds but never bronchial asthma. To God be the glory

No Chance Encounter

The special week of meetings was set aside from studies for students to think on things spiritual and was an indirect way of teaching students to put books aside and refresh their souls. Class assignments and term paper deadlines could easily cause a student to skip his daily devotional time with the Lord. Consequently, morning chapel was part of the schedule for each day of the week.

The name of the speaker would normally be posted on the bulletin board. At times it would be a member of the faculty or a former student who was a pastor and on campus for a day. Also, once a month, a post-graduate student would be assigned speaker. One comment made by a post-graduate made a great impression on me. In his fifteen-minute meditation he said, "There are no chance encounters in life; everybody crosses your path for a purpose. The meeting has been divinely ordained, and when such meetings occur, each has something to give and something to receive." Remembering those words as a guide for each new encounter, I have felt a deep sense of responsibility, a keener awareness that some statement I make could influence another's life, and I would want my words to produce positive results.

No Second Causes

One day in the Vice President's Old Testament Survey class, he wrote on the chalk board a statement that one could write in his Bible. Whether the professor originated the thought, I do not know, and I have seen it in print since then. On the board he drew a large circle and in the center of the circle he placed a dot. The words accompanying the circle would encourage me during the dark days of testing that lay ahead: "In the center of the circle of the will of God I stand: there can come no second causes. All must come from His dear hand."

This statement I would later find written in my wife's Bible as well. Around the outer edge of the circle she wrote the words, "The will of God," and over the dot is written, "Jean." Imagining the hand on a clock at one, she has the word "Health", at three "Joy", five "Sorrow", seven "Blessing", nine "Sickness", and eleven "Trial". That circle and dot comforted her many times in the years ahead.

Book Report

If a student arrived at MTI with little interest in missions, he usually did not graduate with that same frame of mind. Hearing from missionaries who served God around the world, one would have a heart of stone not to be moved by the cry, "Come over and help us." A course in missions was taught by a former missionary to India. He had spent most of his life as a missionary in India, but what impressed me most was his burden for the people of Nepal. At that time Nepal was closed to missionaries.

Most students at that time would remember him as the professor who talked monotone. It was difficult to concentrate on what he was saying, and as I recall, the attendance at the Sunday worship service was lower than usual when he was the scheduled speaker. However, I personally have never been brought into the presence of God as I was after his message one Sunday morning. At the close of his message (given in the same characteristic monotone voice), we could not move. The sense of God's presence held us as if we all stood on holy ground. How long we all remained I can not recall, but we left silently without the usual loud chatter after the service.

A book report was required for this professor's class before the end of the semester. Naturally, the theme had to do with some aspect of missions. Writing a book report was not one of my favorite pastimes. In fact, I had devised my own system in high school when choosing a book. It went like this: I went to the aisle in the library that shelved books dealing with the required subject, then found a book that met three requirements: 1, the shortest in height, 2, the thinnest in width, and 3, the most shallow in depth. That semester, having found one that met these stipulations, I was amazed by the entry date marking the first time the book was signed out, and, though available on the shelf for a number of years, it had been signed out by only a few. The original card was still in use. The author of the book was a single girl who was serving the Lord in a remote part of India. In that small book, and in the providence of God, I read words that the Lord would use to guide my future: "Content to fill the smallest place if Thou be glorified." She could not know how those words would influence my life.

Plucked From the Grapevine

It wasn't until the second semester that I began to notice a student who sat near me in class. She was soft spoken and had a sense of direction for her life. Other students liked what they saw in Jean Roberts, too, and some explained they were trying to get up the courage to ask her for a date. After hearing that someone else was going to ask her for a date after our evening meal, I met her *before* supper and asked her for a date while helping her with her coat.

Getting acquainted, we learned that we had had similar experiences, for while I was struggling spiritually and emotionally in Washington, Pennsylvania, the Lord was working in her life in Johnson City, New York. When she was very young, she received Christ as her Savior and served Him in her local church. She taught Sunday School Class, sang in the choir and in a girls' trio. She too had "gone steady," but she told him that she could not marry him because he had never accepted Jesus Christ as his Savior. Since that seemed to be the only barrier between them, he did what others have done – he responded to an invitation in church to please her. With that obstacle removed, they could be married.

Now, because her pastor had a world vision for the lost, he frequently invited missionaries to speak to the congregation. One such speaker was the founder of a newly established Mission to the Andes. The mission compound was located in Medellin, Colombia, South America. After hearing the challenge to reach the lost in Medellin and the remote areas of the Andes Mountains and plains, she responded, "Here am I, Lord, send me." In those years candidates were often considered by mission boards immediately after high school graduation. They believed that the younger a candidate was, the easier it was to learn another language, so to go to language school after high school seemed logical.

The experiment proved right for Jean. She did learn the Spanish language easily. After completing nine months of language school, along with two other single girls of the same mission, she went into the remote areas of the Andes Mountains and plains with the Gospel. Sometimes they would ride their burros along narrow mountain trails all day to reach a small group of people and share the Gospel. But, because of political unrest in the country and when she grew ill with malaria, she was advised by her mission board to return to the States for college and then continue language study. Teaching children in a Sunday School class had not prepared her for the demands of missionary life and work.

Arriving home after two years in Colombia, she sent applications to different schools that could prepare her for her return to Colombia. What better place than the Missionary Training Institute? In the meantime, the man she dated showed little interest in spiritual things.

We had discovered we both had been reared in a Christian home; both of us had accepted the Lord when young; both of us had been romantically involved in a relationship of our own doing which later was discontinued. Though we were separated by thousands of miles at one time (I in Washington, Pennsylvania, and she in Colombia, South America), the Lord brought us together as students at Nyack, New York. Had I accepted the offer of an education at another college with all expenses paid, our paths may never have crossed. Obviously God was interested in the lives of we two struggling young people, and He delights in guiding those who seek His will.

Permission and Marriage

MTI required permission for undergraduate students to be married before graduation, so Jean and I submitted our request to marry during the summer prior to our senior year. In deciding on a date for the wedding, we had to consider the hectic graduation events, the need to travel on deputation to raise financial support to go to Colombia, and adjusting to another culture. Would it be wise to cram so many adjustments into the same year we were adjusting to marriage? And if we married before graduation, how could we adjust to married life when each class would demand hours of study?

Then there was the financial consideration. Though Jean's home church had been and would continue to pay for her tuition, my G.I. benefits for education had been exhausted. So it was decided: the best date was early June. Furthermore, the glass factory where I had formerly been employed paid above average wages and usually hired extra help during the summer months. So the wedding was planned for Saturday, June 2nd. We planned to be married in Jean's home church in Johnson City, New York. For our honeymoon, we would travel to Lake Erie and then south to Washington, Pennsylvania, where my relatives and friends could meet my new bride. While there, I wanted to apply for work at my former place of employment where I was known and experienced.

All went as planned until I mentioned in Washington that I was going to apply for a summer job at the glass factory. The glass company was not hiring, however, but laying off workers due to repairs. This meant trying to find employment back in Johnson City, New York. It was there that I got a low paying summer job. Though no funds could be set aside for tuition and books, my salary met our weekly expenses, while Jean's sister and husband invited us to live with them. So at the very outset of our marriage, we would have to believe God for our financial needs.

At the end of August, our pastor asked Jean and me and two single girls to speak in the Sunday Evening service. We were all students at MTI preparing for the Lord's work. In order to help us financially, a special "love offering" was received for us. With our share, I had enough funds to pay for my first month's tuition, books and one month's rent for a married couples' apartment. For the rest, we would have to trust the Lord to provide.

Like most college students, we were excited to arrive back on campus. Little did I anticipate what was waiting for us. The Lord's timing is perfect. As I stepped out of the car in front of the building where arriving students register, I heard my name called. It was a student from my home church. We had entered MTI the same fall semester. He asked, "Do you want a job? I quit the summer job I had off campus and will be working on campus this year. I told my boss that I had a friend who may be looking for a job, and he said that you could have it, if you want it. It's a good paying job sanding and finishing floors, from 1:00 – 5:30 in the afternoon and eight hours on Saturday." I went to talk with his former employer and was hired. It wasn't the easiest job sanding and refinishing floors, but the income was enough to support us.

As to the tuition, some of the men of Jean's church were challenged to send to the Treasurer's Office the amount needed for my monthly tuition.

At this early stage of our married life we were learning that when God calls, it is our responsibility to obey, and when we obey, it then becomes His responsibility to provide the ways to meet every need.

We also were learning that God not only *provides* but

also *enables* us to fulfill whatever He calls us to do.

Along the Way

Launching Out

Missionary Conference

Because we werc older than most newly married couples, we were anxious to start a family. After a number of consultations with a doctor, the day came when he gave us the good news that we would be parents. Along with the excitement of becoming parents we would soon graduate from MTI.

In the meantime, Jean contacted the Mission under which she had served and advised them of our marriage, imminent graduation, and desire to serve in Colombia.

She learned that the Mission had since merged with an

older, larger mission, the Oriental Missionary Society.

Because doors were closing in the Orient, the O.M.S.

had decided to extend its outreach to Latin and South

America.

We received a letter inviting us to attend its National

Convention in Indiana where we would meet with the

examining board and get acquainted with its outreach

and requirements. The one requirement which we were

not prepared for was that every male missionary must

serve in a pastorate for at least one year. This news

was a disappointing setback. We wanted to go to the

mission field as soon as we could gather our financial

support. The sooner we got there, the more people we

could lead to Christ.

Perplexed, we were subdued as we sat and listened

to returned missionaries talk about what God was doing

in peoples' lives around the world. Then a soloist sang a new song he had written. His name was Stuart Hamblen. He sang "It Is No Secret What God Can Do." How timely the title at that hour in our lives! It was also no accident that two male delegates from the East Emmett Church in Newton, Kansas, were there. The church which they represented supported missions and missionaries, and needed a pastor. The one who had been serving them had just returned to the mission field.

After examining and subsequently accepting us as missionary candidates, and aware that one of their supporting churches was in need of a pastor, the Mission Board made arrangements for the two men of the East Emmett Church to meet with Jean and me the following day. The four of us spent our time asking and answering questions. The result was a quick trip back to New York to pack our belongings and head for

Newton, Kansas. Our first church service was to be in August 1952.

What I shall never forget is the kindness of the congregation accepting us. We were as green a pastor and his wife as a church could invite and yet they received us with open arms.

Our first Christmas together in a newly built parsonage was like a dream come true. Though Jean wasn't as frisky as she had been eight months earlier, she was forgiven, for in another month she delivered our first child. As it happened, on January 27th Jean had a very difficult delivery. Jean needed immediate attention and the doctor handed the newborn to the nurse. Jean in distress was listening intently for the cry of her baby boy, but there was silence. Suddenly the nurse called, "Doctor, you'd better come quickly and help us. The baby is not breathing, and we can't get him to breathe." Finally, she heard that first cry,

that announcement, "I'm here, Mom. I'm O.K. now.
How is it with you?"

What the problem was or how serious it may have
been, we were never told, but we have always thanked
the Lord that our firstborn was placed in Jean's arms,
and he in his own way let her know he was very much
alive.

Newton Kansas

East Emmett Church

The year passed quickly. If we had not had a call,
it would have been so easy to remain at East Emmett
Church as pastor. But we had to concentrate on raising
financial support. A list of things needed for the first
five-year term on the field had been mailed to us. We
would need to arrange our own itinerary as soon as the

necessary funds and equipment were promised and we would go to language school in San Jose, Costa Rica.

The funds needed for equipment and financial support was larger than we imagined. And when it came time to say good-bye to our church, this dear fold had promised to meet fifty percent of the money we would need each month for a five-year period. We were overwhelmed. The remaining fifty percent was promised by supporters in Jean's church and my home church. To have all our support met in four months was certainly the Lord's provision for us.

Language School

With our support promised, the next challenge was to get reservations on a flight to Costa Rica. But with all flights booked until after the first week in January, we had to arrive a week late for the start of Language School. Jean being late was not serious, for she would be taking a refresher course, however, I had a much greater challenge. I knew only one word in Spanish and that word was "no" which is pronounced the same as in English. So during our flight Jean taught me my first new word: "si" meaning "yes." By the time we arrived in San Jose, I had that one word mastered!

My first day in grammar class overwhelmed me. Not only were the other students one week ahead of me, but all had studied Spanish in high school and college. Most knew how to speak Spanish almost fluently and had a sizable vocabulary. However, while I was the only student learning elementary Spanish, the other twenty students had to unlearn much of what they had been taught in the States. Sensing that I might be overwhelmed by the gap that existed between myself and the other students, the grammar class teacher made a special effort every day to encourage me. She would tell me not to be concerned because I was not par with the other students. She would say, "Right now it seems very confusing to you, but one of these days it will all make sense. Everything will come together." And so it did.

For Jean the three-month refresher course was all she needed. Her recall of Spanish vocabulary was quick, and she was speaking Spanish fluently. Since she no longer needed to attend class, she found a lot more time to spend with our first child. This time also helped prepare physically to give birth to our second child in July. This time all went well in her delivery.

Unrelated to childbirth, an inexplicable incident occurred. It was during the middle of the night when she awakened me and said that she felt sick and thought that she might faint, and when she came out of the faint, she was drenched. She had been sweating profusely, and she was extremely weak.

After a few more episodes in the following weeks, we decided she should see a doctor. For a few days she was subjected to several tests, and all the results were negative. We were advised to return to the United States since there were no further medical tests available there, and this we did in November.

Return

Jean's tests in the United States did not give us answers. Believing it was not wise to return to the field just yet, we notified all our supporters to discontinue supporting us and use the same money to support other missionaries. Being of good health, I would be able to support the family.

We had no idea how dark the days would be as a result of our having to return from Costa Rica. A few people who had been friends now shunned us because we were no longer missionaries. Before leaving our home churches we had been praised for our calling, now some supporters believed we had let them down. One went so far as to say that the reason Jean took ill was because she was out of the will of God. They forgot that Jean had become ill while in Costa Rica not in the States. Nevertheless in spite of Jean's illness we felt the peace of God. It was His peace that held me fast during these trying days.

I began to struggle with my submission to God to become a missionary. I wondered if God had taken me to the field to test my submission, and then having passed the test, allowed me to return to the United States. Though I had the peace of God within me, I still experienced a dilemma. Knowing that the reason for our return may not be associated with my surrender to be a missionary, I still was unable to understand why we had to return to the States when the need for missionaries on every field was so great. I explained my dilemma with a missionary who was a guest in our home a few years later. He asked me, "You haven't quit, have you?" Had I lost interest in the work of the Lord? I answered, "No." His words were used by the Holy Spirit as a "wake-up call." As I searched my heart, I realized that I had not been putting my heart into the ministry. I wasn't giving it my best. In fact, it was as though being in the ministry was a lesser call than being a missionary and that was not so. Both places of service are necessary and important in order that the lost might be reached.

New Assignment

In April, Jean's pastor invited us to attend the annual conference of our denomination to be held in May in Wisconsin. Occasionally a church would need a new pastor, and at the conference the vacancy would be filled if a qualified individual was available. As the Lord would have it, there was a vacancy. After a thorough session before the Examining Board, I was accepted and assigned to a church in Pascoag, Rhode Island. There I would serve for two years to comply with the conference policy, after which I would be given another two-year assignment.

The next assignment was in New Bedford, Massachusetts. Then, after serving two years in New Bedford, the church and we could mutually agree whether I would remain their pastor or accept an invitation by another congregation to be their pastor.

Since we had arrived in the U.S. from Costa Rica, our doctors had tried to find out the cause of Jean's fainting spells. None of the doctors nor any of the tests offered a probable cause other than it might be her nerves.

In the meantime she began to have a dull headache that never let up, day or night. We started to keep records to see what preceded these fainting incidents. Eventually our records showed that one would occur every month accompanied by a severe headache. As months passed the headaches got more severe, so Jean determined to go to the doctor.

New Advice

The doctor suggested a probable cause and solution. The cause of her headaches was "her nerves" and I should take Jean to New York City as often as I could so the two of us could "pop the cork" (get drunk) to relieve the tension. If that did not help, he would advise that I resign from the ministry, move to a quiet region of the country and get a job where there would be less stress on Jean as a pastor's wife.

We left his office feeling sorry for him, for his advice was the best he had to offer. We knew that "our help cometh from the Lord" and not from the contents of a bottle.

Now all life did not stop for us because of Jean's headaches. She would never allow that to happen. In fact, very few knew of her condition because she never mentioned it. One of the things she never permitted in our home was self-pity for any reason. So, life went on.

During this time, we lived in a parsonage in New Bedford which was a traditional colonial home with high ceilings and an attic above the second floor. Now for an adult an attic can be fascinating. One can find things in a suitcase or an old cardboard box that bring back memories. But to a child, an attic is just plain spooky, and even though that child might be dying to know what is up there, he would never go there alone. Hearing one day that Daddy was going to go up to the attic, our son asked if he could go along. The steps leading to the finished flooring in the attic and the burned-out light bulb that I had not taken the time to change would teach me another lesson.

The entrance to the steps of the attic was a door near the end of the hallway. After opening the door, there were two steps to a landing, then a right turn and five or six more steps up to another landing, and then another right turn and up more steps to the attic floor. The day was dreary and there was little light on the first two steps and landing when I opened the door. Taking my hand, my son asked "Daddy, we aren't afraid of the dark are we? Jesus is always with us." Pleased with his statement of faith, I answered, "True, Honey. We don't have to be afraid. Jesus is always with us."

By then we had reached the next steps and were standing in total darkness. Suddenly I felt a little hand squeezing and holding tightly to mine and the words, "Daddy, I think I am getting a little bit afraid."

How true in any age. When our pathway is bright, we boldly say, "I am not afraid," but when the clouds darken the path, we too, "get a little bit afraid." His response taught me an unforgettable lesson. When my way is dark and I find myself getting afraid, I must hold tightly to my Father's hand.

Climbing up to the attic, I was not afraid. I knew that in a few steps beyond the last right turn we would enter the light. I knew it because I had been there before. In the same way He has gone before me. He knows what lies ahead. Just as I held the hand of my child when he was afraid, so He holds the hand of His own. He will never let go.

Summer School

As a graduate of the Institute I was still on its mailing list. I received a brochure announcing the dates of Summer School and the subjects being offered. The subject, "The Family," held particular interest, for I felt weak in counseling skills. Though it meant leaving home at 2 a.m. Monday morning and driving five hours to campus, I enrolled to take the course. Since it was an accelerated course, the class was from 8 a.m. until noon Monday-Friday. The afternoons and evenings were spent preparing the next day's assignment. When Friday noon arrived, it was right to the car and a five-hour trip home.

Driving alone gave me a lot of time to think about what I had learned, and my thoughts were not always pleasant. I realized I had not been the sweet, loving, caring, understanding husband I envisioned myself to be. In fact, I wiped away tears from my cheeks as I thought about how wrong I had been.

Now I could have arrived home and never told Jean what I had been thinking about as I drove. I could have decided secretly that I would try to be a different person, a better husband, but that was not what I needed to do. What I needed to do aggravates that which lies deep within each of us, my pride. Pride keeps me from saying the two most difficult things to say to anyone: "I was wrong" and "I am sorry." These words admit imperfection and that is the last thing a proud person will do.

Over the years I have observed escape routes that are so subtle that a person may not even recognize his guilt. Instead of saying, "I am wrong," one is most likely to say, "Oh, I thought you were talking about something else." And instead of saying, "I am sorry," the guilty is more likely to prepare a peace offering. If a wife is wrong, her escape route may be to cook for her husband his favorite meal or dessert; when he is wrong his escape route may be to buy her flowers or candy or run the vacuum cleaner. Yet what a spouse wants to hear and what needs to be said is "I was wrong."

In the spiritual realm, instead of admitting "I am wrong" (I have sinned), someone may join a church. Instead of saying "I am sorry" and asking for God's forgiveness, one may contribute financially or become a worker in the church. In fact, pride keeps many sinners from turning to Jesus Christ for salvation. Yet the Bible clearly states, "For by grace are you saved through faith; and that *not of yourselves*: it is the gift of God, not of works, lest any man should boast" (Ephesians 2:8, 9).

Truly, confession is good for the soul, but it is not for the purpose of clearing my conscience. Our marriage was not all clear sailing. Just because we were Christians did not mean we would live happily ever after, that we would never disagree on any issue, or that we would never have a day when we would have little if anything to say to each other.

As a single girl Jean had survived two years in another country. She had been faced with life-threatening situations. Sleeping in a hammock at night was a way of life. She had adjusted to a diet totally unlike any she had been served in the United States. So having to depend upon a man for survival was like needing three legs in order to ride a bicycle.

Often she would ask, "Jim, why is it that you are always right and I am always wrong?" Now that was a loaded question. No man in his right mind would try to answer it! To do so would be digging a bigger hole, but to be silent would be admitting she was right. I have often said in the days since her home going that though I am looking forward to being with Jean again, I can foresee our conversation. After reminiscing about our times together on earth, I can almost imagine her saying, "Jim, there is something I want to go over with you. While waiting for you to come, I went over the records here of our heated disagreements." Then, pulling out a long list, she will say, "Do you remember when you said I was wrong and you were right? You need to get down on your knees and admit "I was wrong" and "I am sorry." As my sons will readily attest, she will not allow me to admit my guilt in a whisper. Should I try to do so, she will sternly say in the tone and volume of that familiar Sergeant, "I can't hear you!"

Perhaps these remarks are familiar. Those who can relate will readily admit that when a heated argument arises in a marriage, it has a great impact on the Christian's life and home. When life is not as sweet as it should be between spouses neither feels like reading the Bible, praying, attending church, or talking about the Lord. So not only is there distance between husband and wife, but distance between the person and the Lord. Broken fellowship between us and the Lord creates an atmosphere of unrest in life and home.

Surely there is a Biblical solution to this common situation. The answer is in the Word. The remedy is so simple that couples find it can work if they agree not to let anything interfere with their fellowship with the Lord. Maintaining an unbroken fellowship has to be a priority. I discovered that when I want to please the Lord more than winning a major difference of opinion and Jean wants to please the Lord more than being hostile, the result is a tranquil home. The solution we found to those opposing positions was to go together to the Lord in prayer and invite Him to be a third party. Proverbs 3:6: "In all thy ways acknowledge Him, and He shall direct thy paths." Holding hands as we knelt together with a sense of His presence was a wonderful way to remove hostility and mellow our attitudes. As I surrendered my position to the Lord, and she surrendered her position to the Lord, He was able to direct us. We each gave up what we wanted for what

God wanted. The amazing truth is that God's plan is not only the perfect one but also produces a natural and spiritual bonding of hearts. Surrendered wills on bended knees creates a happier marriage.

Along the Way

Discovery

Tumor

We had driven our car for five years, and it was ten years old. Looking for a newer one was an adventure. We were not impressed with what was available in the local area, so we traveled on Saturday to Providence, Rhode Island, and visited some of the used car lots there. At last, we found one that we liked at an affordable price. However, I felt reluctant to buy the car that day. We planned to return Monday morning to make the trade.

On Sunday afternoon we totaled all our financial commitments and found that they could be met. The only thing that might increase expenses would be the health of our three boys. Our third son was born in New Bedford. Would we face doctor bills and prescriptions? We made no decision about the car that day.

It was sometime during the night that Jean woke me saying she felt faint, even more severe than earlier fainting. I called the doctor's office and was told that the doctor would see her in the morning. Though she had not mentioned it to me before, she told the doctor that since her last visit she had severe pain behind her left eye. After examining the eye, he called the Pratt Diagnostic Clinic in Boston to set up an appointment for Jean as soon as possible. His only explanation for the call was that he felt further examination was necessary.

A few days later an arteriogram at the Pratt Diagnostic Clinic in Boston revealed a tumor behind the left eye. For seven years the fainting and headaches had been diagnosed as "nerves." I told the doctor about the previous erroneous diagnosis, and he said that I should not fault the other doctors for their conclusions. If he had not arranged a second arteriogram thus discovering the tumor, he too would have sent her home saying it was her nerves.

June 30, 1961, was the date set for the tumor to be removed. Jean was thirty-two years old. Because the tumor was located so deep and the surgery urgent, only half of the tumor was removed with the possibility of removing the remainder within a year.

Payment

Prior to her discharge, my primary concern was the success of the operation. We had been advised that complications might arise as a result, however, none of these happened. Now my thoughts went to the hospital bill.

When she was admitted to the hospital, we were asked how we would pay the medical bill,

Did we have any medical insurance coverage? Since the answer was "no", when Jean was discharged, arrangements would need to be made at the finance office for payment. The news about our financial need which was increasing daily went out to our friends and family. This daily increase was the primary thought on my mind one morning as I drove to the hospital to visit Jean. I was singing "A Child of The King" for I often sing when driving. "My father is rich in houses and lands; He holdeth the wealth of the world in His hands; of rubies and diamonds, of silver and gold. His coffers are full, He has riches untold." Then I prayed, "Lord, I believe your coffers are full, but that is not helping me down here." His response came to me, "Trust me and I will open those coffers." In a few days I began to receive money from around the country, money from people I have not met to this day.

So believing I needed His direction about spending the money, I prayed for wisdom. I decided to pay off all our monthly commitments with the money received, leaving us debt free, then put the remainder towards the hospital bill. You cannot imagine how I felt when I walked out of the Finance Office after Jean was discharged. The only monthly bill we had was the hospital bill, and it was within one dollar of the total we had been paying on our former monthly commitments.

With joy welling up within me, I said a very foolish thing to the Lord, something that embarrasses me to confess. I said, "Lord, it would be so nice if you would send in the total amount of this hospital bill so that I wouldn't owe a cent to anybody." Immediately, I felt rebuked, "Look, I promised to meet your need, not to put you on easy street!" "Oh Lord," I said, "I'm sorry. Please forgive me." I wonder how often I am not content with the Lord meeting my needs because I want to be living on easy street.

Our family memorized Matthew 6:25-34. We learned that God does not owe us a new car, home, well-paying job, or perfect health. He has promised to provide for the necessities of our lives, such as clothing, daily bread, and shelter. Everything else is added blessing.

Home

After six weeks in the hospital, it was good to have Jean home. Her appearance had been dramatically changed. In order to perform the surgery all of her hair had been removed, and at the time of the operation a nerve that was responsible for left eye movement was damaged, resulting in that eye being held stationary by the nose giving her a cross-eyed appearance.

Adults can accept change, knowing it is a small price to pay for life. However, her appearance was terrifying to our two and a half-year-old son. He rejected his mother and would cry for "his other mother" or for "his real mother." This was heartbreaking for Jean, for he would not allow her to come near to him. When she tried to approach him to pick him up, he would scream and run the other way. It was not until her sister brought a wig for Jean to wear that our son could see she was his "real mother."

Being rejected by her baby boy was only one of her problems during this year. For some reason she was afraid that she was losing her mind. At these times I would hold her on my lap in a rocking chair in the center of the dining room and rock her like a little baby. Sometimes it would take a couple of hours for me to convince her that people who are out of their minds are not aware of it. They are not capable of such reasoning. Furthermore, "God hath not given us the spirit of fear, but of power, and of love, and of a sound mind" (2 Timothy 1:7).

That first year was endless for Jean for another reason. Had not the surgeon said that he might remove the remaining half of her tumor within a year? So day after day she waited for the mail to see if an appointment was forthcoming, and with every passing day, her anxiety increased. Finally the appointment arrived.

The doctor apologized for the long delay after hearing of her anxiety. He explained that during the past year he had presented Jean's condition to his colleagues at the conventions he attended. Some suggested a wait-and-see attitude, while others opted for removal of the remaining tumor. He finally made his decision by asking himself, "What would I do if Jean were my own wife?" He decided to let it alone. Perhaps it would lie dormant or break down completely. It might grow again at which time another operation would be in order. However, if we wanted it removed then he would give us the names of some surgeons who would do it. "As for me, count me out," the doctor told us. I responded, "Doctor, we prayed and asked the Lord to direct you in your decision, and we accept it."

(One of the things that has puzzled me over the years is why some Christians have said to me, "Pastor, I am praying that the Lord will guide you in your decision," and then they will not accept the decision or question it. In reality they are praying, "Lord, would you please tell the pastor what I think he ought to do so that I can cooperate with him and give him my support?")

Meanwhile, during this year and the years to follow, Jean was praying daily secretly, as I learned, "Lord, please let me live long enough to rear my three boys."

After They Are Gone

About 4 p.m. on a Wednesday afternoon, a man knocked on our door, a total stranger. He introduced himself and asked to come in. His visit seemed urgent.

He explained that a year earlier his wife's leg needed to be amputated just above the knee due to gangrene. Now if her other leg was not amputated, she would die within three weeks. He asked me to come and visit with her. He prepared me for the reception I might receive from his wife. Always in the past when a pastor visited their home, she would announce to him, "I am a home Baptist. I stay home and mind my own business." This was her way of saying that pastors were not welcome there.

I told him I would visit her the next day. That evening, at our mid-week prayer meeting, I requested prayer for this wife and my visit to their home. I needed divine wisdom.

On Thursday afternoon, I found her seated in a chair with her infected leg propped up. Her husband introduced me to her as the pastor of the church where they attended when they were newlyweds fifty years earlier. She did not greet me with the expected rejection because the Lord had softened her heart in answer to the prayers of the night before.

The two-hour visit was joyful. I sensed immediately that I was there fulfilling the providence of God. Both husband and wife were open to conversation about spiritual matters. They each proudly showed to me their parents' Bibles which they cherished. Many verses had been underlined and there were notes written throughout the Bibles.

Each had a parent who had been a Sunday School teacher, and by the verses underlined it was evident they had rightly divided the Word of Truth. They had enjoyed their first year of marriage and were active in the church, singing in the choir. But, sometimes, one's happiest days are interrupted by some unexpected event that changes the course of a life. One of their parents became very ill. The usual course of action was to call the family doctor and the pastor to come to the home.

The doctor who had examined the patient was being paid for his services just as the pastor arrived. In fact, the pastor had witnessed the payment.

That pastor encouraged his ill church member with comments, scripture and prayer. When it was time for the pastor to leave, he asked to be paid for his visit. Seeing the shocked look on their faces, the pastor said, "You paid the doctor for his services, didn't you?" The pastor was paid, but the two sharing this with me in their living room had become so disheartened and angry, they decided not to go to church again. Now fifty years later they admitted they were wrong. They could have gone to another church, but they were so distraught by what had happened, they had given up on Christianity.

When the time was right, the Holy Spirit prompted me to ask, "Wouldn't you both like to return to the Lord this afternoon?" They both said, "Yes." After fifty years far from God, this husband and wife poured their hearts out to Him. As I listened, I knew that nothing I had said or done that afternoon brought about their change of heart. What the Lord had privileged me to witness was the answer to *prayers uttered years before by godly parents.*

Just as Jonah ran away from God, so sometimes do those who have grown up in Christian homes and been taught the truth. Yet God never gave up on Jonah. What an encouragement to grieving parents to pray for their wandering children! God who prepared the universe and all that is in it took the time to prepare a great fish for one runaway- Jonah. I marvel that Jonah did not cry out to God the moment he was swallowed. Most would cry out to God immediately, but Jonah was stubborn. He was not going to give in though his life was in danger. It took three days before Jonah prayed. What a place to have a prayer meeting, in the stomach of a whale! No cushioned pew there. When a man swallows bad fish, he gets sick to his stomach, but for Jonah, it was just the opposite. A healthy fish swallowed a bad man, and got sick to its stomach.

God can use extraordinary means to rescue a "Jonah runaway." When we read the story of the Prodigal Son, we can sympathize with the father who stays home waiting for his runaway son's return. One of the hardest things for Christian parents to do is to stand back and wait for God to work. Naturally they want to go after the child and bring him or her home, if possible, but sometimes that child will run away again. When a child runs away, parents can pray and believe that God is able to reclaim their runaway. God knows where every runaway is. It must be the Holy Spirit that changes the heart and leads them to repent. God's timetable may be such that His work will be accomplished after the praying parents are gone.

Incidentally, that woman did have her leg amputated and spent the next three months in a nursing home where she was a wonderful witness until the Lord called her home.

A – B – C

Hard Decisions

It was a hard decision to make and I faced it every May, which did not make it any easier. The congregation in its annual meeting had voted to ask us to remain as pastor and family for another year. My response to this invitation had to be decided in a few days. Attendance at church was increasing as were the finances. The inside of the church had been refurbished and the outside painted white, restoring its

New England appearance. During the five years of our stay, our hearts had bonded. We and the congregation working together was more than I could ever have asked for.

In the meantime I had received other requests to serve as pastor from other congregations. They too needed a response from me at that same time. I remembered a principle I had learned from one of my former professors: when making a critical decision, write down the positive things that would lead you to say "yes," then write down all the negatives that would lead you to say "no." Now go over the two lists, weighing the pros and cons. When that is done, crumble the lists and throw them into the waste basket. Get down on your knees and pray, "Lord, what would you have me to do?"

My answer came the day of the deadline as I was in my study. The words that came to my mind were,

"Other sheep I have which are not of this fold." The answer was clear. I notified the congregation that I would not be returning, and then contacted the church in Shamokin, Pennsylvania, that I would accept their invitation to be their pastor.

A farewell service was hastily planned in New Bedford with several of our friends in the church participating. My best lasting impression of that evening was a duet sung by a mother and her son. The words have stayed with me over the years: "Many things about tomorrow, I don't seem to understand. But I know who holds tomorrow, and I know who holds my hand."

My first day in the pulpit in Shamokin would be Sunday, June 2, 1963. The date was easy to remember. It was the date of our twelfth wedding anniversary. My stay at the church in Shamokin would be brief, but a distinct part of God's plan. The move was not of my making, but God's. His plan would lead me from A (New Bedford) to B (Shamokin) that I might be where He could then lead me to C. This He accomplished in a most unusual way.

Plan C

What one word of advice do we hear most often to improve one's health? Is it not the word, "Relax?" Everyone knows we need to relax, however, we may not agree about the best way to do so. For one, it may be sitting quietly while reading a book, and for those who do not like to read, it may be some sports activity such as swimming, riding a bicycle or golfing. My favorite way to relax had always been to take a ride in the car in a rural area. Taking a road I had never traveled made a trip extra special.

To break the routine of traveling the same highway to do hospital visitation, I drove down a gravel road one day, trusting my sense of direction to finally arrive at the hospital parking lot. Passing a few homes a road took me east, but, because of six-foot high field corn obstructing my view around the bend, I slowed down. The corn was turning brown, and fall was on its way. The Lord interrupted my thoughts with the words, "Here is where I want you to build a church." Months later I learned that God was laying it on the hearts of other young men throughout our country to start independent, fundamental, Bible-believing churches. At the time I thought I was the only one who had received such a call!

I told Jean about my experience on the way to the hospital. She agreed that we should follow wherever the Lord would lead. I called the District Superintendent of our conference and a church business meeting was called. The Superintendent announced my call to begin a new work and my resignation as their pastor. The

District Superintendent assured them that he would supply an interim pastor immediately so that the work there would not suffer.

My resignation meant that we would need to vacate the parsonage, and there would be no financial support coming from the church. I would forfeit all the monies I had contributed to a pension plan during the past nine years; Jean and I with our three boys would now need to "believe God" to provide a way for our needs to be met. Some described our actions as "stepping out on faith", while others questioned the wisdom of such a move. Why leave such security when you have a family to support? However, obedience was our responsibility; provision was God's.

I had two questions to answer. Am I an obedient Christian walking in all the light that He has revealed to me? Am I in the center of God's will, exactly where He wants me to be? If we were in the center of His will, then it was God's responsibility to supply our every need.

When my resignation became public, we received many phone calls offering assistance. A gentleman who lived in the same city block offered housing in what is called in the area "a half-double." The half he had been using for storage could be cleaned out with the help of a few men and we could move in and live there rent free as long as we desired.

Though my resignation had been made public, no details had been given as to where this new work would be located. A few families who were not members of the church but had been attending the Sunday evening service called to say that they had been praying and asking the Lord for a ministry like the one the Lord was leading me to begin. One family in particular had returned to the area from Chicago and was searching for a church. The husband had just recently accepted the Lord in Chicago and had been advised by friends before leaving to find a church where he would hear the Word and grow as a new Christian. It was in this family's home that we met on a Wednesday evening for prayer, seeking guidance. In attendance were 13 adults and 4 children. Only two were members of my former church. This was exactly as I had requested; I did not want the move to be considered a church split by the community.

Some of the men in that first meeting were acquainted with other Christians in the area. They volunteered to inquire about the availability of a place to hold our church services. By Friday, arrangements had been made to rent the facilities of a nearby fire hall for Sunday services and a prayer meeting on Thursday evening. The first meeting in the fire hall on Sunday, October 3, 1965 was attended by twenty people, including the children. Adding to the excitement of that first service was a man and his wife accepting Jesus Christ as Savior at the close of the service.

Having acquired a meeting place, we had to organize a committee to search for property in a desirable location to build a church. At the same time, we decided that Jean and I would be responsible for our own support so that a Building Fund could be instituted through free-will offerings. There would be no other means used to raise money.

With a Building Committee of five men formed, a search for property began throughout the area but with no success. I had not told the committee of my earlier experience near the cornfield. Finally, I suggested to the men that we make a visit to the home of a man who lived in nearby Paxinos and was beginning to sell some of his farmland. I had been told that the owner of the farm was always home in the evening, so I saw no need to call and set up an appointment.

When our committee arrived at the man's home, I introduced ourselves to the wife who came to the door as men who were looking for property to buy. She directed us inside to where her husband was sitting. When I told him who I was and that we were looking for property to build a church, he said, "I know just the place to build a church." Pointing, he said, "Right out there on that corner." It was the very corner where the Lord had said to me, "This is where I want you to build a church!"

After some discussion, a price was quoted for two acres. We were promised the first choice on the purchase of an adjacent third acre as well. The next step was to go the bank and get a loan. Naturally some collateral was needed by the bank before a loan could be granted. Again the leading of the Lord was manifested. Though not a prerequisite for serving on the Building Committee, most of the men were property owners, and a few were willing to put up their homes as collateral.

After the land was purchased, a sign was erected to announce "The Site of the Paxinos Bible Church," and because it was the latest church news in the area, a picture was taken of the sign and published in an area newspaper. The picture caught the attention of a man who had constructed industrial buildings in the state. He was retired and living in the area. After reading the accompanying article, he came to our home to put before me a proposition. I did not share his proposition at that time with anyone. It was a proposition which appeared to be an answer to prayer, especially since I was then employed by Montgomery Ward as a part-time worker. He promised to erect the kind of church building we wanted at no cost to us. He would pay for the materials and construction as long as I agreed that the church would be the denomination to which he belonged. He had wanted a church of his denomination in that area for some time.

Now that was the second time that I had such an offer. The first was an education with all expenses paid if I would consent to being a pastor in a particular denomination. Now it was a church building – mortgage free. Just imagine! A newly-build church completely paid for at the outset. I could quit my part-time job; the Building Fund would not be needed, so the congregation could assume our full financial support.

Now the denomination to which he belonged was by no means considered liberal. However, I felt I had to decline his proposition because it conflicted with what I believed the Lord had asked me to do. This was a test for me. It involved me – nobody else. Would I obey the Lord and travel the hard road, or would I take the easy one and say, "Yes"? It has always been more important for me to obey the leading of the Lord than to do what others think ought to be done.

An Unbelievable Plan

With property purchased, we concentrated on the funds to erect the building. In the meantime, however, Jean and I felt that it was asking too much of our friend to expect to continue to live rent free in his half-double house. Furthermore, living near the newly-acquired property for the church would be much more convenient. So, as often as we could, we began looking for available housing near the church property.

Finally we drove past a new ranch-style home located on a dirt road. Jean and I with the three boys peered into all the windows that we could reach. It was obvious that the home had never been occupied; the dirt had not even been pushed back against the foundation. A week later we drive past the house again, but still no sign of life and no "For Sale" sign. So I inquired where the tax collector lived. I went to her home and she gave to me the name and address of the owner.

The timing was all of the Lord. When I visited the owner, she explained the circumstances. The house we were interested in was to be the first of many. She and her husband planned to build a development and their closest friends were planning to buy the first home. However, a few days before the sale of the house, her husband had died suddenly of a heart attack. Because of the shock of his sudden death, she had put the sale of the house to her friends on hold. Soon after that, the wife of the intended buyer fell and severely broke her arm, changing their plans to buy. Another major factor at the time of our visit was that the owner was scheduled soon to have a serious operation. She would feel much better if she knew before her operation that the house and property were sold.

Now she, too, through reading the newspaper, knew of our plan to build a new church. She also knew from our conversation that afternoon that we did not have the amount required for a down payment for the loan. She suggested an unbelievable plan. She would allow us to rent the home with the option to buy. We would also be responsible for the home owner's insurance, property tax, and any regular repairs or those caused by recklessness. The monthly rent payment would be deposited in an escrow account under her name and ours. After we had paid enough rent in the ensuing months to be equivalent to the down payment, she would pay the down payment with the escrow and the balance could be mortgaged. The agreement was drawn up by her attorney, making it binding and legal. So it was that we were able to move out of the city and nearer to the place where the church would be built.

Contractor

With the blueprint of the church building finalized, contractors were asked to submit a bid. Though all estimates to build were about the same, it was not difficult to make a choice. The one contractor said that it had been his desire since being in the business to build a church. We had not been able to get a bank loan to construct the entire church building until we had twenty thousand dollars invested in the initial construction as collateral. However, this contractor said he would be willing to build in phases as we raised the money. As construction was nearing the end of the first phase, we still needed three thousand dollars to complete the basement and have it undercover. The money in the Building Fund was being paid out as rapidly as it was coming in; the balance was almost *nil*. It was then that I remembered something I had heard in college: "There are no chance encounters. There is a divine purpose when your life crosses the path of another." Could it be that the gentleman who volunteered to construct the church was one of those "divine appointments"? The only way to know was to go to his home and discuss it with him.

As a builder he understood the urgency to have the first phase completed to protect what had been constructed, and when I suggested a personal loan from him to the church, he made no comment but excused himself and left the room. When he returned he was dressed in a different outfit and asked that I go with him to the bank where he suggested that I remain in the lobby while he went to talk with the bank personnel. Fifteen minutes later he returned and told me to go to an inner office to sign a paper. He had set up a loan for the church for the amount of three thousand dollars and had co-signed it. By so doing he was helping the church establish credit with a bank to prepare us for that larger loan we would need in the future. Chance encounters? Never!

Another factor concerning the building contractor was his willingness to allow qualified men of the church to do some of the interior construction. The men the Lord provided were bona fide in their profession: the electrician, carpenters, plumbers, audio technician, painter, and many handy-men like me. Many worked three to four hours in the evening after their regular day's work and also returned on Saturday.

The major loan was granted and the building completed with just a few hitches along the way. It was a blessed day. Later, on the eighth anniversary of the church, the mortgage was burned.

Lessons From Rural Life

Praying for the Black and White

Living in a rural area with all the various sounds on a warm summer night was quite a contrast to the sounds we heard while living in the city. In the city we were used to the sounds of an ambulance, fire truck, police car or metal colliding with metal. Now we heard the bawling of cows, peepers, frogs at a nearby pond, heat bugs, crickets, and occasionally a hoot owl. But the sound I heard one particular night I could not identify. It was a scratching sound and seemed to be outside our open bedroom window. With the spotlight turned on illuminating the yard, I could not see what could make such a noise. Puzzled, I went back into the house, turned off the spotlight, and went back to bed. Just as I was drifting off to sleep, the scratching sound resumed. Again I got up and turned on the outside light but I didn't see anything. It wasn't until the third episode that it occurred to me that perhaps the sound was not outside but directly below us in our basement. So I walked very softly across the hardwood floors, down the basement steps, and turned on the basement light. There was a black and white skunk in a window-well where a galvanized shield was installed. What I had been hearing was the sound of the skunk's claws drawn down across the galvanized shield as it leapt to get out.

What should I do? The skunk had been trying to get out for over an hour and was getting weaker with every leap. If I frightened it and it let loose its lethal weapon, the house would not be livable for days.

Going back to bed I did that which I had never done before or since. I prayed for a black and white skunk. I prayed, "Lord, would you please give that skunk enough strength to leap out of that window-well and be on its way?" When I awakened in the morning and checked the window-well, it was empty. I learned from that experience a simple but important truth. You never trouble God when you take to Him in prayer the things that trouble you, be they large or small.

An Awkward Experience

In time, each person finds himself in an awkward situation. For a woman it may come as a question from a close friend. How can she tell her dearest friend that her new dress makes her look fat? She doesn't want to send her home in tears. So she says, "That color really looks good on you."

For Jean and me one of our most awkward moments happened when my parents were visiting from California. We did not get to see one another often. Almost all of our contact was by phone. So to have them visit with us was a real treat. There would be so much to see and talk about. Furthermore, for our children to see Grandma and Grandpa face to face was important. Photographs can not bind hearts together like an old-fashioned hug.

Our awkward moment centered around a picture. Without a doubt it was a most striking picture of Jesus. Though it was the familiar depiction, it was created in an unusual way. The picture was laminated onto an elongated piece of pine framed by the bark on the outer edge. My mother asked, "Why isn't that beautiful picture of Jesus in a conspicuous place in your living room where all your guests can see it?" She had discovered it hanging out of the way on a wall that could not be seen from the living room.

Jean and I looked at one another. We didn't want to sound critical with our answer, nor did we want to embarrass my mother for asking the question. Reluctantly we told her, "We do not want our guests talking on the way home about the beautiful picture of Jesus hanging on our living room wall. We want our guests to see Jesus in us."

We sometimes sing, "Let the beauty of Jesus be seen in me." That beauty is the result of dying to self so that He might shine through our lives. This has remained our earnest desire and prayer.

A Ewe and Its Lamb

My schedule I endeavored to keep was to study in the morning, and then do visitation in the afternoon at a hospital, nursing home, or private residence. One day the Lord taught me a lesson as I was on my way to visit patients in the hospital. It was warm enough to drive with the car windows down, always a treat after having the car windows up during the colder months. Driving on the main road from our home to the hospital was always relaxing. Generally there was not much traffic, and I could take in the beauty of the distant valley and mountains. What was different that day was a flock of sheep that I was accustomed to seeing on my way to the hospital.

Now because my visit was not urgent and there was not any traffic, I pulled the car off the road to watch the sheep grazing. I did not know the actual number of sheep grazing, but I was drawn to the many little lambs. It seemed that they were everywhere, each near its mother and exercising its vocal cords. They all sounded alike to me.

There were a number of ewes each with a baby lamb at its side. The lambs sounded as though each was trying to outdo the other. As soon as one lamb finished its "Baa", another started. I watched as a sheep at the top of the fenced area bolted and ran full speed down the hillside, dodging other sheep until it reached the lamb that was nearest my car. Out of all the lamb's cries, that mother, a hundred yards away, heard the cry of her own offspring and ran to its aid. When the mother arrived and stood silently by, the lamb stopped calling for it was no longer afraid. I finally left this idyllic setting and made my visits at the hospital.

While I had been at the hospital, my wife had received a phone call from a near-by neighbor whose son was a bed patient in their home with advanced cancer. The parents had opened their home for the remaining days of their son's life for they knew their daughter-in-law had all she could manage with the care of her younger boys.

Because it would be another hour before our evening meal, I walked to the neighbor's home. Since I was new in the neighborhood, I introduced myself to the parents, son, and daughter-in-law. The son, though in his thirties, was thin, pale and very weak. After hearing his testimony of his born again experience, I realized that he was anxious in spirit. Undoubtedly, his concern was for the future of his wife and three small boys. Then, too, what would he have to face before the Lord took him home?

The incident of the sheep came to my mind and allowed me to minister to this young father dying of cancer. I told him what I had seen on my trip to the hospital: the grassy hillside where many sheep with their lambs were grazing, the darting and zigzagging of a mother ewe when she heard the lamb's cry and ran down the hillside to stand at the side of her lamb. Though I did not hear the conversation between the mother and its lamb, I imagine it something like this, "There is no need to be afraid. I am here."

I reminded him that the Word of God refers to us as sheep. Jesus even called his disciples, grown men, "little children" in the upper room before His crucifixion because the disciples were facing the unknown and were afraid. That little lamb had cried out for help because it was afraid. It did not know which way to go to get out of its predicament. The only one that could help in such a crisis was the one who loved it, and that one responded to its cry.

I said to the young man, "The Lord hears your cry as one of His own and will hasten to your side. You are one of his sheep and you are under His care." The reaction of that Christian father was similar to that of the lamb. He stopped calling for help, for help had arrived.

In hindsight, something else transpired that afternoon that did not occur to me at the time. For instance, when the mother arrived at the side of her lost lamb I didn't hear a sound from her, no sound that might have been a scolding. Silence can be a message of the grace of God. We scold our children when they disobey, but when a sinner calls upon Jesus to come and save him, a lost sheep, He doesn't scold him for all his sins. Instead He receives him and makes him one of His lambs, "a babe in Christ."

Tommy

It would be a new experience for me, but one I often recall. The mother and dad with their three sons had moved from the outskirts of Chicago to our community. For her it was moving back home, but for him it was therapy. Due to the stress of his job and their son's handicap, the father was recuperating from a nervous breakdown. He had even contemplated suicide. But, while still in Chicago, he had accepted Jesus Christ as his Savior. He had been advised to attend a church where he could grow spiritually and so he began to attend our Sunday evening services with his family.

Living just two blocks away from the parsonage with two sons near in age to ours, the boys began to play together. Their third son, however, never joined in play. He was mentally impaired. Now the parents did not hide him from the public, but he needed constant supervision. In fact, the day came when he had to be admitted to a nearby state institution. It was a traumatic decision to make.

Visiting Tommy at the institution was extremely difficult for the dad. Seeing other children with similar disabilities tore at his heartstrings. I had often passed the institution and seen children under supervision playing outside, but I had never driven onto the premises. The day came when I was invited by the parents to go with them as they visited Tommy whom I had never met.

As we drove in to the institution, I saw the well-kept grounds and buildings. Before we got out of the car, we noticed some children playing nearby. Seeing guests had arrived, they ran stumbling towards the car, squealing and laughing as they came. The sight and sounds overwhelmed the dad.

Observing his reaction, I said to him, "Bob, you have it all wrong. The ones to feel sorry for are those who are riding down that highway with sound minds but unsaved lives. These who are here are not accountable for their actions; they do not understand the difference between right and wrong. Jesus said, 'Suffer the little children to come unto me, and forbid them not: for of such is the kingdom of God.' Mark 10:14. These children will be in Heaven someday while those out there, unless they get saved, will be lost for all eternity. I feel sorry for those out there."

Just a few weeks before this writing, I watched a mother pushing a young girl in a wheelchair and shopping for groceries. The young girl's arms and legs were bent in unnatural positions. Her head was leaning slightly to one side. Her mouth was twisted. As I felt led of the Lord, I put my hand on the mother's shoulder and said, "Your daughter has a bright future." With a puzzled look she asked, "Why do you say that?"

I answered, "The Bible says the day will come when your child will be given a new body and a new mind when she gets to Heaven."

"Do you really think so?" she asked.

"Yes, I do." A smile of hope and relief came over her face.

Mark 9:43 says, "...It is better for thee to enter into life maimed, than having two hands to go into Hell." Those who have not the mental capacity to be accountable for their actions in this life will be with Jesus in eternity. Yes, to have a child mentally deficient and bound for Heaven is far better than having one of sound mind unsaved and bound for Hell.

The story is told about a man who complained to his brother about their other brother. It seemed he had always been a slow learner and as he got older, he got many things confused. After many years of listening to these complaints, the one brother could take it no longer. Finally he said, "You know, you and I ought to be thankful our brother's brain was not put into your body or mine. The brain he has was not *his* choice." No person can ever feel superior to another, everyone must recognize that the ability to learn and achieve is a gift from God.

Freedom May Be Disastrous

One beautiful fall day seemed to possess its own mystique; the blue sky, perfect temperature, and low humidity gave me a new zest for life. In fact, it so affected my emotions, I would have been willing to give the world away if it were mine to give. Wanting all creatures to feel the same joy and sense of freedom, I decided that our parakeet should be treated to a limited outdoor excursion. Up to that day, its freedom had been limited to inside the house. The parakeet had learned at an early age how to open the cage door, so it went in and out at will. As the only bird in the house, it had its own flight pattern and places to land. When we wanted the bird back in its cage, we would take the cage to it with the door open and say, "Go into your cage, Tippy. Go into your cage," and she always, without any coaxing, would hop right in.

"Free as a bird" was our parakeet. But we know that a bird is not free. Like all living beings everyone is the prey of someone or something else. The game bird is the prey of the hunter. A small house bird can be at the mercy of the elements.

We took our parakeet in its cage just outside our back door. In a few minutes she opened the cage door and hopped around the outside of the cage. A short time later she surprised us by flying up to the rain spouting. This didn't alarm us. We put the cage up to the bird and said, "Inside the cage, Tippy. Go in your cage." But instead of entering her cage as she always did, she flew across the street into a wooded area and out of sight.

Our whole family went searching and calling. We tried to warn her, but she refused to return. We called out her name, but our warning call to Tippy went unheeded. Evidently our call to Tippy was not accepted as loving, but a desire to put her back into the cage and under our control inside our home. If Tippy had only listened! That night the outside temperature dropped too low for a house bird to survive. Tippy was free, but it cost her her life.

Many a person has reached the age of freedom from the restraints of Christian parents only to become the prey of the devil, who is "going about as a roaring lion seeking whom he may devour." It seems that the devil's favorite prey is that one who has been sheltered in a Christian atmosphere. To that one he suggests, "Throw off all these restraints. You're on your own now, so do as you please. It is your life. You are free at last." He never warns the tempted that a wrong choice could make him more captive than he ever knew growing up. Yes, one may free himself from the restraints of home, but one can never free himself from God's restraints. His standards are still binding until this life is over, and no one is free to disobey God at any age.

And to those who have sought freedom outside the will of God, those who love you are calling "Come home. Come home."

Times of Testing

A Difficult Decision

The year was 1973. It was a typical summer filled with church activities. The only unusual thing was the way Jean would occasionally stop, stare, swallow three or four times, and then continue what she was doing. At the time I thought it strange but did not ask questions. Because we had started early one morning and had one of those non-stop days, we agreed to call it quits around 10 p.m. At 11 p.m. I was awakened by

Jean shaking violently. It had been 12 years since her first brain tumor operation and before that she never had such a seizure. That stare and swallowing I later learned is called a mini-seizure. (The violent seizure is called a Grand-mal). Because it was the first of many, I was terrified. After she quieted down, I called our family physician and explained what had happened. It was midnight, but he told me to come to his house. He gave us samples of the medication, Dilantin. "Bring her to my office first thing in the morning," he said.

The next morning after examining Jean, he suggested that we see a neurologist. It was evident that the brain tumor was growing again. Because the results of her first brain tumor operation had been so successful, we contacted the same surgeon we had seen before. An appointment was set for September.

After consultation with him and many tests, the tumor's return was confirmed. This time, however, an operation would be more difficult; the tumor had wrapped itself around the area that controls movement, speech, and sight. He made it clear that if Jean did not have the surgery, she would die. However, because of the location and size of the tumor, there was a chance that Jean might not survive the operation. Jean's forty-third birthday was November 6th. The operation was scheduled for November 7th. She would be admitted in the hospital on the morning of her birthday. Since the surgeon had moved his office to Holyoke, Massachusetts, we planned to arrive at Brattleboro, Vermont, on the fifth, stay overnight, and then travel south to the hospital in Holyoke.

The outcome of the operation lay heavily on our minds as we began our long drive. Our conversation while traveling and eating supper was just chit-chat. Neither of us wanted to think or talk about negative things. Finally that night, we slipped into bed, having prayed together as we always did before sleeping. Turning out the light, we were silent. There was no way of knowing each other's thoughts, but I knew what I was thinking. Would this be the last night we would lie side by side on the earth? The next night she would be in a hospital bed. What could I say at such a time?

Finally Jean broke the silence. "Jim, the Lord hasn't said a word to me about the outcome of this operation. I have asked Him over and over again to give me a word of assurance from the Scriptures, but he hasn't done so. The one thing I must say though – I have no fear. For all these years I have struggled with fear and the Lord has delivered me." I could not assure her that the second operation would be as successful as the first, for I, too, had not received such assurance, but I rejoiced in her deliverance.

Holding hands, as we often did while going to sleep, silence again enveloped the room, each of us struggling with our own thoughts. It must have been near midnight when I finally drifted off to sleep.

We both awakened at daybreak, for we were early risers. We were not able to eat breakfast, so we left the motel and arrived at the hospital for Jean's 9 a.m. admission. Though it was her birthday, there was no celebration.

The operation itself went as planned. When I first saw her in the I.C.U. at 4 p.m., she said, "Well, we made it." Those first ten minutes of visitation were exciting. The surgeon said that he had been able to remove only the new growth. The one difference with this tumor was that it was vascular and some blood vessels were very large.

For the next few hours I visited with her for ten minutes on the hour. At 7 p.m. I was permitted to see her again. This time I noted that her speech seemed to be slightly slurred. I planned to tell the nurse on my way back to the family room, but she was called away before I could do so. At 7:30 p.m. a nurse came to the family room to tell me that Jean had run into some trouble and they were taking her back to the operating room. The surgeon had been called and was on his way.

It was not until later that I learned that her slightly slurred speech a half hour earlier was the first sign of a hemorrhage. The swelling after the partial removal of the tumor had caused too much pressure on several large blood vessels.

After what seemed like an eternity, she was returned to the I.C.U. This time her condition had drastically changed. She was now in a coma which would last for a number of weeks. Joshua 1:9 and Psalm 46:10 were now the anchor for my soul. *"Have not I commended thee? Be strong and of a good courage; be not afraid, neither be thou dismayed: for the Lord thy God is with*

thee whithersoever thou goest." "Be still and know
that I am God."

Because of her condition, she was on full life
support systems. In the weeks to follow she had
many complications: bladder infection, urinary tract
infection, pneumonia, high fever, a tracheotomy, the
withdrawal of dead brain cells which had accumulated
in a large cell of fluid over her left eye. After the fluid
with the dead brain cells was withdrawn, a cap of the
same material as an ace bandage was placed over the
area in an attempt to stop the leakage of the fluid. This
was performed several times, but to no avail.

I was told at the time that the brain does not replace
cells that die, nor do the remaining living cells take
over the task of the dead ones. The function that the
dead cells had performed was no longer operative.
Because of the many dead brain cells that had been
withdrawn, the conclusion of the surgeon was that

Jean would remain in a vegetative state and never know anyone. On two different weekends, when I had returned home to preach on Sunday, the hospital called my home urging me to return immediately, because they believed they were losing Jean. She could not maintain her blood pressure. I had gone to the home of the friends who were caring for our youngest son and never got the call. By the time I retuned on Monday afternoon, her blood pressure had stabilized. Whether or not medication stabilized her blood pressure I was never told, however, the best medicine made available to man cannot overrule the sovereignty of God.

With the frequent withdrawing of dead brain cells, I was confronted with a very difficult decision. In the light of the prognosis what did I want the doctors to do? Did I want all life support systems to be withdrawn?

At the moment the questions were put before me, the thought to exercise my faith and believe God for a miracle of healing never entered my mind. Would I be intruding on God's will? Did I dare tell the doctor to withdraw all life support systems which would result in her death when on two occasions He had allowed her to live?

In answer to his question I said, "Doctor, during this whole period when Jean has been in a coma the Scripture that keeps coming to me is, 'Be still and know that I am God.' You have said that on two different weekends you thought Jean would die, but she didn't. God brought her back, and I am not going to interfere with His plan and tell you to let her go." With that he said, "I have, as a surgeon, done all that I can do for Jean. I will make arrangements for someone to take over her case." Within an hour, a physician introduced himself and said that Jean would now be under his care. He would do all he could to help her, and "If she should ever recover, it will only be to a point beyond which she can not go, due to brain damage."

By the end of the tenth week she was out of the coma, able to recognize our son when he visited, and was flown home in a small plane.

Home, but for how long?

After being home for a few weeks, Jean was admitted to a nearby hospital for therapy. This was routine procedure after such an operation. At the end of three weeks of daily therapy while I was visiting Jean, I was told that I was wanted at the main office for consultation. There I was told to take Jean home that day. Jean had so deteriorated in her three-week stay; they felt she had only three weeks to three months to live.

Driving home, we were just a few miles away from the hospital when I had to quickly stop the car because

Jean started to have a grand-mal seizure. This seemed to confirm what I had been told at the hospital. As I helped her into our home I had a sickening feeling in my stomach. The operation had not quelled the seizures. Now I would not have a nurse at the end of a hall to buzz or a doctor who could be at her bedside in five minutes. From then on, I would have to trust the Lord and the Lord alone to help me. That was exactly what He wanted. He often removes our earthy props and assistance that we might learn to wholly lean on Him.

For the next three years Jean was not fully aware of what was happening around her. At times I wondered if she understood that I was her husband or even a familiar person whom she could trust. As a result of the hemorrhage following the operation she was not able to talk, read, write, or walk without assistance.

She also had a paralyzed right arm and hand and was incontinent.

Without the help of the ladies of the church, I could not have continued my ministry. Each day of the week one or more would come and care for Jean while I fulfilled my responsibilities. They also volunteered to prepare our evening meals, do housecleaning and washing and ironing. This they did faithfully for a number of years.

Unknown to others at this time, my heart was breaking as I looked at Jean. Inside I was overwhelmed with a sense of guilt. Her physical condition was my fault; I had broken a promise, a promise only the two of us knew, a promise she had begged me to keep just before the operation! "Jim, I want you to promise me that if I don't come out of this unscathed as I did the first operation, you will let me go to be with the Lord." I had had that opportunity but I didn't act on it.

"Oh Jean, I'm so sorry. I'm so sorry," was the cry of my heart as I looked at her.

It was a year or so later that I confidentially shared this guilt with Jean's sister. Her response helped me greatly. She said, "Jim, your decision was based on all the information you had at the time. You believed you were doing the right thing. Now learn to live with that decision." She was right, and it eased my guilty feeling. Since that time, greater assurance has come to me when recalling my decision. It all goes back to the decision we had faced earlier in life about starting a new church. At no time did she then or after question my obedience to God's call. She did not want to interfere with the leading of the Lord in my life, no matter what the cost was to her. I believe she would never have expected me to keep a promise made to her that would conflict with what God was permitting. The doctors had given no hope for her recovery, but twice she had lived before when they thought she would die.

I would have told them to remove all of the life support

systems except that God had clearly told me, "Be still

and know that I am God."

Three Circles

After a shunt was implanted in 1976, Jean did

recognize most of her family and people of the church.

She could say, "Yes, no, chilly, hot, okay, hungry,"

sometimes "bathroom" and later a new word, "weary."

She could repeat after someone, but could not initiate a

conversation. She could not refer to anybody by name.

She could sing just above a whisper the first stanza of

every hymn that we had sung regularly over the years.

Why certain things registered and others didn't I

can't explain. When I took her for a car ride each day,

we traveled the same route through a rural area. Some

things she would remember having seen before and others she could not recall.

One summer day while traveling the route she said, "Jim" and smacked her lips. This meant there was something she wanted to eat, something for which she was very hungry. With that I suggested that she get a napkin from the glove compartment and gave her my fountain pen. I told her to draw a picture on the napkin of what she wanted to eat. With the pen she drew three circles, evenly spaced. Then handing the napkin to me she pleaded, "Please, Jim, please." With that plea I said within, "Lord. I have no idea what Jean is pleading for with these three circles. You dwell in her and you dwell in me. You know what she is asking for. Would You please tell me what she is asking for?" Instantly the answer was given. I turned to her and asked, "Honey, are you trying to tell me that you want a banana split with three dips (three circles) of ice cream?" Joyously she exclaimed, "Oh yes, Jim, yes. Please, please." She had remembered that we would pass a soft ice cream drive-in. I stopped and I got her a banana split. Now only the Lord could have revealed such knowledge to me. Just as I have often delighted in treating my children to ice cream, God delighted that day to treat Jean, His child, to a banana split. Often He blesses us with little surprises.

A Heartbreaking Scene

One Sunday morning I witnessed a heartbreaking scene. As I did every morning, I bathed, dressed, and took Jean by wheelchair to a chair in the living room. I turned on the TV and switched to a channel where she would hear a message from God's Word. Though the church service was not the one she usually watched on Sunday, I didn't search for another because I was pressed for time. Besides, Jean was not always capable of understanding what was being said, so I didn't feel it was urgent to change the channel.

Although I could hear the sound of the TV, my mind was on my preparation for that morning's service and the message that was on my heart. My attention was drawn, however, by the TV speaker's comments about sickness and divine healing. In the course of his message, he stressed that it was the will of God to heal all believers. All sickness, he said, was of the devil and could be overcome by exercising one's faith. "If you have the faith to believe, God will heal you." In the closing minutes of the telecast, he urged all who were viewing by television to "exercise your faith and get out of that bed. Get out of that chair or wheelchair and walk." Just then I heard a noise from the living room. Jean had pushed back the footstool, and her right shoe fitted with a metal brace to the knee had struck the floor. With her feet now on the floor and her left hand grasping the arm rest, she was pushing and leaning forward in an effort to stand and walk. Over and over the speaker challenged the viewers to exercise their faith and get up and walk. At each challenge Jean struggled to stand, but she could not. Finally, in deep despair, she pushed her body back into the chair and closed her eyes. Her body seemed to wilt. I knew she was inwardly crying out, "O God, what must I do to get enough faith for you to heal me? I tried."

During the next few days she withdrew into her own world, showing no interest in anything. She didn't want to view any television and kept her chair turned toward the wall with her eyes either closed or staring into the wooded area across the road. However, once again her short memory would be a blessing. She came out of that experience as though it never happened. This selective memory loss remains a mystery to me. Why an individual with brain damage can remember some experiences and not others takes a wiser person than I.

Healing can and will happen. Why God healed me earlier in my life and not Jean is up to Him. We know that with God all things are possible, but we do not know what He will do. For that reason we should pray and believe God for healing.

Flight from Texas

One of my favorite pastimes as a boy was to cut out and glue together model airplanes. The wood was lightweight balsam. When the model was assembled according to the enclosed plans, there was a thin paper that was glued onto the outside of the structure. While I was assembling the plane, my mind was dreaming of the day when I could be a pilot for a major airline.

In High School I got very excited when it was announced that there was a special assembly in the gym at 11 a.m. A former graduate who had become a pilot for a major airline would be addressing the student body.

During his presentation he described how by the sound of a long or short beep heard over the headset he would know if the plane was going off course to the left. Another beep meant that the plane was going off course to the right. After demonstrating the two different signals, he asked the student body if they could distinguish between the two sounds. The majority thought they could, but I could not hear the distinction between the two sounds. I decided that day I would stop dreaming of becoming an airline pilot. However, I never lost interest in airplanes.

Years later, my son expressed an interest in becoming an airline pilot. I asked him what gave him the idea that he wanted to fly an airplane. He answered, "Dad, every time we went for a ride in the car, we ended up at an airport!" The truth is that not only did I like airports, but also television programs that involved airplanes. Because of my interest, I remember watching a story about two young men whose single engine plan crashed in a remote mountainside region. Though both survived the crash, one was pinned in the plane while the other, though injured, was able to get out. The following day they agreed that the one who was able needed to go for help. Not knowing in which direction to go, he set out on foot hoping for the best. In the meantime, though severely injured and in much pain, the one trapped in the plane was able to free himself a few days later. Knowing the best thing to do in order to be found was to stay near the crash sight, he did not wander. About a week later his friend having found an old logging trail returned with a rescue team.

I like stories that have a happy ending. But as we all know, real life doesn't always have happy endings.

About a month after I heard the true story related there was a knock on our door about 8 a.m. Standing on the porch was a Pennsylvania State Trooper. It was evident from his somber face that he was on a serious errand.

He asked if I knew where a particular family lived in our rural area. Our youngest son had the newspaper route in that neighborhood so I was able to direct him to the home. He told me he had been sent to inform the family that their son had just been killed in a car accident on his way home from work. The son had worked night shift until 7 a.m. and had fallen asleep at the wheel, crashing his car into a small bridge.

Just a few weeks later our son was planning to return from Le Tourneau College in Longview, Texas where he was studying mechanical engineering and taking flying lessons. He had earned his solo and instrumental flying license and made plans to fly home alone in a single engine plane and land at a small local airport around 10 p.m. Knowing the time and date of his planned arrival, I had been watching the weather forecast for a couple of days.

On the day he was scheduled to leave Texas, there was a large weather front that extended from the U.S. and Canadian border to the Gulf of Mexico. It was described as a severe weather front with high winds. Throughout the day I tuned into the weather channel as often as I could. Finally 10 p.m. arrived with no word from our son. At 11 p.m. still no word. During the weather segment of the 11 o'clock news the weatherman reported again, "Severe weather with high winds all along a front extending from the Canadian border to the Gulf of Mexico."

In the meantime Jean had remained up long beyond her bedtime. She was so excited that her son, Dan, was coming home. Finally, trying not to alarm her, I slipped

into our bedroom and knelt to pray. It was near midnight.
Where was Dan? Can that small plane withstand those
high winds reported by the weatherman? Has his plane
gone down in some remote area like those two young
men in the story?

Another hour of testing had come. It all came
flooding back to me. Crying, I prayed, "Lord, when
Dan was just a few weeks old, Jean and I stood at an
altar and gave him back to You. We told You that he
was Yours for You to do with his life as You pleased.
Again I surrender him to You, but Lord, if those high
winds have caused his small plane to crash in some
remote mountainous region, I ask this one thing,
please, please don't let him suffer. If You are going
to take him, take him quickly. And Lord, Jean is so
excited! How am I going to tell her that her Dan won't
be coming home?" In tears I cried out, "Oh Lord, if

You are taking Dan tonight, You are going to have to give to me more grace for I can't handle any more."

As I wept silently at the bedside, the phone rang. Would it be a state trooper saying there had been a plane crash in our area and the pilot was our son? Would they ask me to come and identify his body? Or would it be a doctor calling from a hospital with a similar message? I answered the phone and a voice said, "Hello Dad, this is Dan. I am calling from Pittsburgh. I have been flying into some very strong headwinds, delaying my time of arrival. The plane has been refueled and as soon as I get clearance, I will be taking off and be home in about an hour and a half."

Apparently, God had no intention of taking Dan that night. I was on trial. Did my surrendering Dan to God allow Him to do with Dan as it pleased Him, including death? That night I told God, "Yes." Any surrender, commitment, promise or vow is rather meaningless until it is put to the test and survives. How deep would my surrender be? How long would it last?

25th Anniversary

The Paxinos Bible Church was a test for all of us. As the Lord entrusted the care of His servant Jean to me years earlier, we had been entrusted to the congregation to care for us. When we first started the work, the Lord knew the kind of care we would need in the future. But twenty-five years was a long time and I sensed a restless spirit in the people and a desire for a change of pastor.

Now I write this without the least bit of animosity. One of the darkest days of my ministry was the twenty-fifth anniversary of the founding of the church. Twenty-five years at anything has special significance. If it is twenty-five years of marriage, it is extolled as the Silver Anniversary. If a business establishment has served the community for twenty-five years, there may be a month-long sale of celebration. During the twenty-five years of the Paxinos Bible Church, many had knelt at the altar and had prayed for salvation. Some were moms, dads, sons, daughters, brothers, sisters, parents or friends. A man and his wife, the first converts at the first service held in a nearby Fire Hall, were present. And when the ushers came forward to receive the morning offering, I half-expected one of them to hand me a card signed by the members of the congregation, thanking me for the years of faithful service. That did not happen. In fact, not one of those shaking my hand when leaving the service said, "Thank you pastor for your willingness to obey the Lord and step out on faith to begin this work. I was saved here."

I went home truly downcast. It seemed as though those leaving the service were afraid to speak a word of encouragement lest I interpret the words to mean they wanted me to continue as pastor. Yet I was not surprised. I suspected that some members wanted a change of pastor. Church attendance was lower. I understood their desire for change, and had Jean's health been good, perhaps we would have served at several churches during those twenty-five years.

The prospects of being invited to pastor another congregation were almost nil. How could I candidate? What congregation would consider one at my age whose wife was disabled and unable to participate in church activities? We were too young to retire and receive full Social Security benefits, and medical bills were high.

Throughout this period, I was pleading with the Lord to reveal to me His will. Twenty-five years earlier the Lord had spoken to my heart and said, "Here is where I want you to build a church." Now I found myself praying, "Lord, would you please speak to me and tell me what You want me to do? I sense what man wants me to do but I want divine orders. I know, Lord, my reasoning may conflict with Your plans, so guide me. You know that I have preached and firmly believe that if You call, You will provide. Since I obeyed Your call years ago to begin this church, You have provided for our every need. I will trust in Your faithfulness to continue to provide if I follow where You lead."

My dilemma lasted until deer hunting season which began on the Monday after Thanksgiving. On the first and second day of hunting, I did not see a buck. On the third day, knowing that I had to pick up Jean from the Adult Day Care Center at one o'clock, I knew that I could not hunt after 10 a.m. If I did, I would have not have enough time to field-dress a deer, drag it out of the woods, load it into the trunk of my car, take it to a butcher to be processed, go home, get out of my hunting clothes, freshen, drive ten miles and be on time.

So at 9 a.m., I did something that I would not advise anyone else to do. Because I had not heard from the Lord about whether He wanted me to resign or remain, I prayed, "Lord, if You want me to stay, would You please send a deer (any kind will do) through these woods at 10 a.m.?" After all, doesn't Psalm 50:11 say, "The wild beasts of the field are mine?" At 9:45 I began a countdown: 9:50 to 9:59 and then seconds, 15, 10, 5, 4. At the count of 3, I heard a rustle of the leaves on the upper flat. Two seconds. One. Just then I saw the head of a doe come into view at exactly 10 a.m. She walked slowly down into a ravine, crossed the bottom, and went up the other side and out of sight.

For the next five years I clung to that experience in the woods. I kept thinking of a statement made years earlier by the Vice President at MTI, "Never doubt in the dark what God has revealed in the light."

Finally Jean reached the age of sixty-five and was eligible for maximum benefits under Social Security. She was in very poor health. The brain tumor had been slowly growing again and had grown extremely large. Her neurologist could not understand how she could have such a large tumor in her head and still be alive. It was then that I told the members of the Church Board that I was resigning as pastor and would advise the congregation of my decision.

Along the Way

A New Beginning and a New Ending

Retirement

While assisting an interim pastor for the first few months, personal concerns now needed attention. It seemed urgent to have our wills brought up to date and a Living Will drawn up for each of us. When we had Jean's Living Will made, we did not realize how important it would be in just a few months.

Having informed the congregation of my retirement as pastor, a farewell supper was held at the Fire Hall where the first church service had been held almost thirty years earlier. It was truly a memorable evening. The following morning with the car packed, we started out on a trip to Clearwater, Florida. There we planned to enjoy a few weeks of vacation with our son and family. We also planned to look at some homes to see if it would benefit Jean to move south. Certainly she would be able to enjoy the warm winter months. The winter we had just lived through in Pennsylvania was said to be one of the worst in years.

Driving away from our home left us with mixed emotions. We had put our home up for sale and a sign stood in the front yard. Having lived thirty years in one residence, it was difficult to part with the familiar setting of years of memories. Our sons were grown, but memories of teasing, laughter, and tears were still fresh in our minds. Conditions compelled us to move on. What the Lord had in store for us we did not know, but we had peace, knowing He had faithfully directed our steps in the past.

After a brief rest from our travel, our son took us real estate shopping. We wanted to get an idea of what homes were available and at what cost. What we could buy would depend on the sale price of our house and when it would be sold. Normally it would take four months or more to find a buyer in our area of Pennsylvania.

Is This the Road to Heaven?

Just four weeks after leaving Pennsylvania, Jean was taken to the emergency room of a nearby hospital. After examination she was admitted with pneumonia, and nine days later she was transferred from the hospital to a nursing home for therapy and recuperation.

There at the nursing home we would continue the practice established at the outset of our marriage

– prayer together at bedtime. Originally we had taken turns, but now only I could lead in prayer. After I prayed, I would kiss her goodnight and always say, "Well Honey, we are now one day nearer Home," and with excitement in her voice and her good hand lifted heavenward, she would always exclaim, "O yes, Jim, yes!" With all her physical limitations she was always aware of her Blessed Hope. The surroundings of the nursing home reminded me that the time to lay hold of our assurance is when we are mentally capable of doing so.

While visiting Jean, an incident happened that made this so evident. A patient in a wheelchair would often pull herself down the hall while singing familiar hymns. She would go down one side of the hall to the nurse's station, turn around, and then go down the other side. The impression I got from the hymns she sang was that she was a born-again Christian. Then one evening, about the usual time, her pattern changed. She pulled herself along by taking hold of the handrail and paddling with her feet, but there was not singing for she was on a mission. Stopping at the open door at each patient's room, she would look in and call out, "Jess (her husband), are you in there?" Not getting a response, she would call out again, "Jess, are you in there?" Then she would go to the next room and repeat the call. The sound of her voice weakened as she got farther away. When her voice grew louder, I knew she was returning on our side of the hallway. I will always remember when she paused at the doorway of the room Jean occupied, looked in, and called out, "Jess, are you in there?" The call was so desperate I wished I could answer, "Yes." On she went until the sound of her call could no longer be heard.

A few days later I heard her voice again. I had spent Sunday morning with Jean, listening to some gospel messages over the Christian TV Network and helping her with her Sunday dinner. I left and went to my son's home to have dinner with the family. After spending a few hours there, I returned to the nursing home to spend the rest of the day with Jean. When I opened the main entrance door, I started down an incline towards Jean's room. At the bottom was this same dear woman in her wheelchair with her hand on the railing and feet pushing on the floor in an effort to ascend. When I reached her side, she looked up at me and asked, "Mister, can you tell me if this is the road that leads to Heaven?" That ramp, to her, was a road. Was it the road to Heaven? No, of course not, but there was no way I could explain the plan of salvation so she could comprehend and respond. It was too late for her to understand her need. But the songs she had sung and her desire to go to Heaven gave me a glimmer of hope that perhaps she had indeed known "the way" earlier in life when her mind was well.

One of the most helpless situations a pastor can experience is when a person is so ill or incapacitated that the pastor has no way to communicate. But more hopeless is the one who can communicate but has no interest in spiritual matters.

Over the years I had two similar situations, but with opposite responses. The first experience was with a retired friend, one I had known for a number of years. His wife had died earlier, and he had no immediate family. So when word reached me that he was a patient in a local hospital, I went to see him immediately.

As always, my concern was primarily for the spiritual need and then for the physical. God often puts people on their backs physically that they might see beyond the ceiling of their room and recognize the frailty of their lives and this need to get their spiritual life in order. After talking about our common interests (always a good place to begin), I gradually led our conversation to spiritual matters. I mentioned to the patient the number of years that God had given to him and that it was time to be certain that he was ready to meet the Lord. I tried to help him gently to see his need to accept Christ then. Instead he asked, "Jim, what is the weather like outside?" Recognizing he wanted to change the subject, I answered his question.

Just then a nurse came into the room to ask how her patient was feeling. He said he was feeling better but a little earlier he had lost his lunch. She told him that he should have called for help; that was the reason the nurses were there.

After she left the room, it seemed the opportune time to read Scripture and have prayer. I had other commitments so two hours passed before I finally arrived at home. Before I could remove my coat, the phone rang. My next door neighbor had seen my car pull into the driveway and was calling to tell me that she had just received a call from the hospital. Our friend to whom I had witnessed just two hours earlier had suddenly died of a heart attack.

Whether he had accepted the Lord after I left, I have no way of knowing. But this I do know – he had full presence of mind two hours before eternity.

Now the second incident. I received a phone call about a middle-aged man in an area hospital. I had known Ed for some time. The first time we met was years earlier when I had conducted the funeral of his twin brother who had been killed in an automobile accident. Within the past three months I had also conducted the funeral of his dad where he had been present. Ed had been admitted to a nearby hospital with severe head pain. There the test revealed that the cause was vasculitis, a rare vascular condition. Medication did relieve his distress, so he was discharged from the hospital. The next day, however, he was stricken again with overwhelming head pain. He would then be admitted at the larger hospital in the area. When visiting with him I talked about his need to be saved and left some tracts and The Daily Bread for him to read. On my return visits I asked him if he had read the tracts and he said, "No."

I know that pain can be so severe or a person can be so ill that it is impossible to read. Not knowing why Ed had not read the literature I left with him, I prayed just before I drove out of my driveway, "Lord, help me reach Ed today."

When I got off the elevator in the hospital, I looked into the faces of a number of the family members and saw deep concern. I asked how Ed was doing. They answered, "He has been in a deep coma for some time.

His wife is with him." I left them and walked toward his room praying, "Oh Lord. Please help me."

When I arrived at the door to his room, it was only partially open. What I saw at a glance was his wife her face down on his bed and her hand reaching up to hold his. Rapping on the door I said, "Hello Ed. Reverend Tarr."

"Hi Rev. Come in." His wife, not believing what she was hearing, jerked her head up. At that moment I knew that what I needed to do, I needed to do quickly. I walked to his bed, took his hand and said something like, "Ed, you are a very sick man. Now I know that on my way home I may be in an automobile accident and die before you do, but on the other hand, you may die first. Would you like to ask the Lord to save you just now?" "Yes" was his answer. Realizing that he might never have prayed aloud, I said, "Ed, repeat this prayer after me. Dear Jesus, be merciful to me a sinner. I know you died on the cross for me. Forgive me of all my sins and come into my heart and save me." Realizing moments were fleeting, I prayed as I always did when one was saved, "Thank you, Lord, for saving Ed just now. You promised that 'He that cometh unto me I will in no wise cast out.'" Though my prayer was brief, I sensed that before my prayer had ended, Ed had slipped back into that coma. Two hours later, without regaining consciousness, Ed was in eternity.

It was a year or so later when Ed's wife became ill and was taken to the area hospital. Again I was contacted by a member of the family and visited with her.

I was glad to have the opportunity to see and talk with her again. I asked permission to speak of the events on the day of Ed's death. I went over each detail. I asked, "Had Ed been in a coma before I arrived that day?" Answer, "Yes." When I rapped on the door and said "Hello Ed. Reverend Tarr," he said, "Hi Rev. Come in." She answered, "Yes." "Now this is the most important part. I want to be certain that I remember exactly as it happened. He repeated a prayer after me asking the Lord to save him and immediately slipped back into that coma without responding again and died two hours later?" She said, "Pastor, that is exactly as it happened, and as Ed prayed and asked the Lord to save him, I too, prayed and asked the Lord to save me."

Since that experience I have a new appreciation of what transpired on Mt. Calvary when one thief said, "Lord, remember me when thou comest into thy kingdom." Jesus answered, "This day thou shalt be with me in paradise." A few hours later it was so.

As to my two friends, each made a decision just two hours before entering eternity. I heard one pray for forgiveness and salvation. What the other did in those last two hours I do not know. I leave the matter with God.

I must not forget my responsibility in these two incidents. To my knowledge, I was the last one to tell these two that they needed to accept Jesus Christ as Savior. Though I lost two friends, I have peace knowing that two hours before eternity I did all I could to prepare them to meet the Lord.

HOME

I received a call from a realtor in Pennsylvania that there was a buyer for our home. Papers needed to be signed; the house vacated. Arrangements were made to keep Jean at the nursing home at personal expense until I returned.

In Pennsylvania I immediately contacted the Realtor. With the Bill of Sale finalized, the gigantic task of packing and sorting furniture and personal belongings took a few days. It was decided that my two sons who lived in Pennsylvania would transport our belongings to Clearwater where they would be put in storage until a suitable house could be found.

Physically exhausted by then, I did not think it was wise to drive alone back to Florida. It would be too easy to fall asleep driving, so I asked my grandson to share the driving. We will always remember the last four hours of the trip. We were both so tired we were "slap-happy." We laughed until we cried. Laughter is a wonderful gift from God.

Jean returned to my son's home two days before our forty-fourth anniversary. It was good to have her home! We talked about our lives together, recalling our many experiences, and knowing it was time to plan for the future. Many times during the past twenty-two years it had seemed certain that God was going to call Jean home, but time after time He brought her back. In

1974 she had been given three weeks to three months to live. In 1983 a CAT scan had revealed a large, growing brain tumor. The neurologist told me at that time that Jean had at most two to three years to live. It has been said, "Live as though this were your last day on earth, but prepare for the future as though you were going to be here for another one hundred years." None of us know how long or short life will be, and we need to know that we have made a commitment to trust Christ for our redemption.

House shopping seemed like a new experience, not having done so in thirty years. With the money from the sale of our Pennsylvania home, we knew what price range to consider. Though many houses fit that category and were attractive, they would not meet our needs. Because Jean had to be transported by wheelchair, extra wide hallways were a necessity.

Meanwhile Jean's health continued to deteriorate and on July 8th, she became a Hospice patient. Our search became all the more urgent. With the help of realtors who were friends of our son, we were taken to a condominium for sale that had not been listed on the open market. It was an end unit on the first floor overlooking a small lake. The hallways and doorways were wide and the bathroom had easy access. The master bedroom was in a perfect location. I could help Jean sit up in bed, open the curtains and she would have a perfect view of the lake – an ideal setting for a bed patient.

We decided to paint the walls and ceilings and have the carpet cleaned before moving in the furniture. The day after the carpet was cleaned Jean and I drove to the condo. The half-hour trip was exciting and we were full of anticipation. The carpeting would be dry, and we could plan the placement of the furniture in each room.

Just inside the front door was a tile floor four feet wide and thirteen feet long. At the end of the tile floor the carpeting began. With Jean still in her wheelchair, I locked the wheels. I removed my shoes and walked toward the bathroom. Just as I returned, Jean began falling head-long out of the wheelchair. When her head hit the tile floor, the sound was like that of a firecracker. Her eye glasses punctured her skin just at the eyebrow and blood was flowing down her face. I ran and got some paper towels and ice cubes from the refrigerator and held the ice over her eye to slow the bleeding. Then I lifted her from the floor and placed her back into the wheelchair. I handed her the paper towel with the ice and told her to continue holding it over the cut while I went for more ice. When I returned, the blood was flowing as before because she had not held the ice over her eye.

I knew that I needed to get her to the emergency room, but, as I was about to turn the wheelchair around to get out the door, I noticed that her left shoe was lying on the floor off to the side. I thought that her shoe had simply come untied. It wasn't until after she had ten stitches (five inside the cut and five on the outside) and was waiting for a prescription that it dawned on me what had caused that whole episode. "Honey, did you try to take your shoe off as I did so you wouldn't soil that cleaned rug?" She said, "Yes!"

The doctor's final instruction at the Emergency Room was to return on Saturday afternoon to check the wound for infection. That Saturday there was no sign of infection, but I told him that she was not acting like herself. The doctor felt that if a minor concussion had occurred as a result of the fall, it would right itself in a few days. If she had sustained a major concussion, nothing could be done because of the tumor, so we returned to my son's home.

When Sunday morning arrived, we saw in Jean major changes. She would not open her mouth to eat, and pushed the food away and refused liquids. By day's end she had slipped into a coma.

The family was notified of Jean's condition. Those who could, came. For the next few days Jean remained in a coma. The help from Hospice was invaluable. Such care and concern was far beyond our expectations.

On Saturday morning I called the funeral director in Pennsylvania. We had purchased a burial plot and made plans years earlier. What we needed was advice about getting Jean's body back to Pennsylvania for burial when the time came.

By noon things began to change. Jean came out of the coma. When her sister and sister's grandson arrived at 4 p.m. from Texas, she was very alert. What a turnaround!

Sunday morning was a time of rejoicing. At mid-morning our one son took our other son to the Tampa Airport to fly back to Newark, New Jersey. Jean's sister and grandson began their trip back to Texas late Sunday morning. That afternoon when we placed our small granddaughter in the bed with Jean, Jean was very responsive and kept patting her little arms. By early evening she took a few sips of Ensure, but, because she had not eaten for a full week, it didn't seem wise to give her too much at first.

Monday morning was more exciting than the day before. She was alert and bright. I explained to her that she had not eaten for a week and to get her strength back she would have to begin eating again. "Are you ready to get going again?" She smiled and said, "Yes." So I gave her one-half can of Ensure.

Because this Monday was Labor Day, September 4th, our son, Jim, took his family out to enjoy the holiday. It was about 11 a.m. when they left. (I had been keeping records of times and dates for years.) At noon Jean drank a whole can of Ensure and wanted to take a nap. I could see that she was getting tired and suggested that we take a nap together. Over the years I learned to take a nap when she did, knowing that I might be up all night watching over her. Before lying down, I decided to wash our laundry. So I told her I would be right back. When I returned, I leaned over to kiss her, and her arm reached up as though she wanted to put it around my neck. Bending my head, I took her arm and put it around my neck and saw a strange look on her face. I knew that something was very wrong. I ran to the phone and dialed the number for Hospice in the event of an emergency. It was 1:30 p.m.

In a short time, a nurse arrived. Checking Jean, she said, "She is going."

"What do you mean?" I asked.

"She has started the dying process," she responded. For the next two and a half hours her blood pressure slowly dropped, stabilized, and then continued to drop.

As the Lord would have it, our two sons and family returned about 4 p.m. and learned of their mother's physical change. Since the grandchildren were home, we felt it fitting to have them stand by her bed and recite together Psalm 23 and 91, which they had memorized. If she heard them recite the Psalm, it pleased her, I'm sure.

Our son, Jim, took his Bible and read aloud many portions of Scripture. If she could hear at this point, as some believe she could, I know the Word was a great comfort to her. As the minutes slipped away, her breathing grew slower and slower. Finally, Jim, sitting on the other side of the bed, mouthed the words to me, "She is going."

During all of this time, I was holding her left hand. Her right arm and hand were paralyzed. Jean and I often held hands, since the time we were dating. She always pressed her fingers as deeply into mine as she could, and that is the way I held her hand. I felt she might subconsciously know I was with her. She had told me years earlier that she always felt safe when she knew I was near. When it seemed she had taken her last breath, I continued to hold her hand until I felt the Lord had taken her hand from mine and said, "Welcome home my child. Welcome home." At long last she touched the One she loved so much.

When Jim said, "She is going," it brought to my mind the comment of a pastor in his radio message. Referring to life as sailing on the sea of life, he reminded the listeners that when someone says, "She is going," they should not forget that on the other side they are saying, "She is coming. She is coming." Later as I recalled the words, "She is coming," I envisioned the reaction of my father-in-law who usually referred to her as his Jeannie. I could hear him calling from Heaven's shore, "Over here Jeannie, we're over here." I could almost hear my mother-in-law say to Jean, "Jean, I want you to meet your brother Billy. You were just two years old when Billy died of rheumatic fever. I know you were too young to remember him." (What a day it will be for those parents whose child died at a young age and for children to meet their siblings!)

One of our sons when he was very little explained how he thought people might find each other in Heaven. He said, "Daddy, if you die and go to Heaven before I do, I want you to stand right beside Jesus so I will know where to find you." Yes, Jesus will be the central figure in all of Heaven and we will see Him.

Funeral

Tuesday morning, September 5th, was the beginning of a new chapter in my life. I would no longer speak of "we" or "us," but "I." Years earlier, when Jean was in good health, we had discussed what to do about funeral arrangements. Jean had requested that there be no viewing, and the casket was to be closed. "If people can't come and see me when I am alive, I don't want them to come and look at me when I am dead." Her second directive was, "No flowers. Instead of flowers let them give that money to help a missionary lead someone to Christ. It would be far better for another soul to be in Heaven than have flowers dying on my grave in a cemetery." I wondered what people would think with a closed casket and no flowers. All too often the value of the life of the deceased is measured by the cost of the casket, the amount of flowers, the number attending the viewing, and the number of cars following the hearse to the cemetery.

Long before her death, the Lord had given me an idea. I would place a picture of Jean taken a few months prior to the operation, on an easel beside her casket. I went home alone to find the picture stored somewhere in the condo. When I opened the door, I saw boxes, suitcases, and trunks everywhere. Where would I find the picture? Not in the three trunks. I went next to open the suitcases. Not there. From there I opened the larger boxes. By then a great sense of loneliness swept over me. Crying aloud, I kept repeating, "Lord, it wasn't supposed to be this way. I wanted Jean to sit up in bed and enjoy her meal as she looked out over the lake. I wanted her to enjoy the beauty of Florida." Then the Lord gently reminded me that no beauty in

Florida could compare with what she was now seeing. At that moment the Lord did what no mortal could do. He took my tears and transformed them into beautiful diamonds reminding me that "precious in the sight of the Lord is the death of His saints" (Psalm 16:15).

Jean was 32 years old when she had her first operation. She told me then that her main prayer request was that the Lord would allow her to live long enough to rear her three boys, then ages ten, eight, and two years old. She lived to rear them but never realized when she made that request that almost thirty-three years later her youngest son, a pastor at thirty-six, would conduct her funeral service. How gracious is the Lord! How can I possibly praise the Lord enough? All I can do is, "Glorify the Lord in the fires."

My Turn

Cancer

I had annual physical exams year after year in January or February. It was the test in 1999 that I came close to missing. Why go through it again? The results are always the same. But, with inner prompting, I decided to have the examination one more time, and the test results suggested a problem with cancer. Since my sister had died of bone cancer at the age of fifty-five, another had had a mastectomy due to cancer, a brother and son had a melanoma removed, my test results put up a red flag. Many tests followed and the diagnosis was a tumor.

This would be the beginning of many precious lessons. The hour had come for me to put into practice my faith in the promises of God. I would have to practice what I had preached!

When the urologist told me that I had prostate cancer, my mind went numb. I tried to listen intently when he explained the types of treatment available, my options, so to speak. When I left his office, my mind was in a whirl. I went through what I can only describe as losing my spiritual equilibrium. For the next three days it did not matter where I was or what I was doing. The thought "You've got cancer. You've got cancer," relentlessly repeated in my mind as if played on a cassette tape. Finally I decided it was time to accept my condition.

I remember telling Jean after her first operation that the tumor was not going to determine the length of her days; the Lord would. She was not going to leave this world one second sooner or later than He had planned. (Psalm 13:8, *"The Lord knoweth the days of the upright."* Acts 17:28, *"For in Him we live and have our being."*)

Now at no time did I deny the presence of cancer, but I determined that once again I would "believe God" for my future. The recommended treatment against the malignancy was the implantation of several radioactive seeds. The next step was a consultation with the doctor who would perform the procedure.

In my first appointment, the Lord opened the door to witness. As a pastor, I had always exhorted my congregation never to feel intimidated in the presence of any person, be it an attorney, college professor, physician or whatever. It does not matter who that person might be. The Gospel message needs to be heard by all. So that day I began almost immediately to speak to that doctor about his need for Christ (no chance encounters!). After about fifteen minutes I remembered that the primary purpose of my appointment was to discuss the procedure I would undergo for the seed implant. I had to be wise when witnessing to professionals who perform their services by scheduled appointments. A few days later radioactive seeds were successfully implanted.

All along the way the Lord has provided me with doctors who have been regarded with the highest respect by their colleagues. Some have openly professed Jesus Christ as their personal Savior, while others have made no comment. My prayer has always been that each one would see Christ in my life. As one of my Sunday School superintendents said, "The only Bible that some people will ever read is your life."

911

In 1998 I retuned to Pennsylvania to visit with my older brother from Missouri who was vacationing in our home town. We had not seen one another in seven years. The following year my younger brother, whom I had seen more frequently, was returning home for a short visit, so naturally, I went back to spend a few days with him. On both occasions it was like reliving our younger days. Since my two sons and their families also lived in Pennsylvania, it was an opportune time to visit with them as well. Weekdays I visited with one son because of his work schedule and weekends with the other. While visiting I volunteered to help with any home projects that needed to be done. I remembered how my dad always helped me with home projects when he and my mother visited our home.

With my radiation treatment behind me and feeling physically able, I volunteered on a Friday to spread lawn fertilizer. While working I noticed a pain under my left arm, the same pain I had a few years earlier while helping to spread sealer on the driveway. I decided it was either a muscular condition or my age.

The next day, Saturday, I drove the 100 mile drive to my other son's for the weekend. Five days later, it was back to the Scranton area to help my son prepare for a corn roast. With seventy people expected, there was a lot of corn to be husked. Late in the afternoon we drove to the church to get tables and chairs. As I was helping to carry the tables to the car, the pain I had had a week earlier returned.

That evening I did not join in the fun. I was puzzled by the pain I had experienced. It could not be my heart; it did not fit the signs of a heart attack. But what was it?

I planned to travel to my son's home in Sunbury on Saturday morning. I wanted to be there when he and my daughter-in-law arrived home from State College. However, because there was so much traffic, they decided to stay overnight and drive home Sunday morning.

On Sunday morning, with the whole house to myself, I decided to give myself a stress test (a bad idea!). I could walk freely up and down the steps without anyone asking me what I was doing. So about 9 a.m., I started from the bottom of the steps and climbed up to a landing, made a right turn and up more steps to the second floor. This I did three times at a normal pace. Then I dialed 911! Because I did not have any real stress when the ambulance arrived, I felt somewhat foolish when they closed the ambulance door and started the sirens. All my vital signs were good but they insisted that I have oxygen as a precautionary measure. After what I suppose was a routine examination for a heart attack patient, I was discharged at 1 p.m. with an appointment with a family doctor on Tuesday.

That examination was routine. The doctor ordered a stress test on the following Tuesday. In the meantime I was put on some medication to avoid any surprises. Having had a few stress tests before with good results, I nonchalantly arrived at the scheduled time. It took only a few minutes of walking on the treadmill before I experienced severe pain which was simultaneously recorded on the monitor. I was immediately admitted as a patient. I was at least relieved to know that indeed the pain was real and not my imagination.

Throughout the day I was monitored and other tests were performed. The heart catheterization revealed many blockages, one so severe they would have operated the next morning if I consented. However, because of the rehab needed after surgery, it seemed wise to return to Florida for the procedure. I was advised to have surgery within the next three weeks.

When I was discharged the next day, I was given the results of the tests and instructed to give them to my doctor in Florida, which I did. A few days later, surgery for a triple bypass was set for September 17th.

Meanwhile, local weather stations were reporting a tropical wave that had left the west coast of Africa over the western Caribbean Sea, drifting northwest toward the Gulf of Mexico. I gave little thought to the weather on September 17th as I checked into the hospital for surgery.

Years before when Jean was in the nursing home, the emergency alarm had sounded and the nurse had called, "Tornado warning." As expected, the nurses and staff members hustled from room to room calling out instructions for all to follow. All the patients were to leave their rooms and shut their doors behind them. Those patients confined to bed were pushed out of the room, bed and all, and into the hallway. There we waited quietly for the building to be struck by the tornado. After ten minutes or so of quiet, we were told we could return to our rooms. We had just gone through a tornado "drill."

Years later, as I lay in my hospital bed, I thought I could feel the hospital building shaking violently. I reasoned that the tropical depression I had heard about a few days earlier must have developed into a full-blown hurricane and was making a direct hit on Clearwater. I waited for someone to push my bed out into the hallway just as they had done in the nursing home during the tornado drill. As never before a deep awareness of the Lord's presence and perfect peace flooded my soul. He was so near I felt I could talk with Him. I said, "Lord, if you plan to take me Home just now that is all right with me, but if you have more for me to do (this book?) and want me to stay, that will be all right too."

Actually, the hospital building was not shaking. I was experiencing atrial fibrillation; a condition during which the upper chamber of the heart is not beating in rhythm with the lower chamber, giving a feeling of shaking within the body. Even so, the presence of the Lord and His peace during that time was a most precious experience.

A few days later I became acquainted with my roommate who happened to be one of the largest men I have ever been near. We talked at length the night before I was discharged. He told me that he worked for a very prestigious organization in our country. It was evident that he had a very responsible position with the company. I commended the way he had climbed the ladder of success. Then, as kindly as I could, I pointed out to him that the ladder he was climbing did not reach high enough to get him into Heaven. Jesus said, "I am the door; by me if any men enter in, he shall be saved" (John 10:9), and Jesus also said, "…I am the way, the truth and the life: no man cometh unto the Father, but by me."

He responded by saying, "When I was a little boy my grandmother used to take me to Sunday School and I remember hearing those same verses." I commented that our being together in that room was no accident. God had brought us together that I might tell him that he needed to accept Jesus Christ as his Savior.

It was already past 11 p.m. and I told him that it was my custom to pray before I went to sleep. I asked if it would be all right if I prayed aloud for the both of us. His response was, "I'd like that." The next day while waiting for my son to take me home, I had prayer with him again. I pray that our conversation remains in his mind even to this day and that he has found Christ.

More to Come

Now though I had been treated for prostate cancer in June and had had triple bypass surgery in September, there was more to come. At the beginning of November, I became very ill. I tried to doctor myself but was losing ground. So giving in and going to my primary doctor, I was diagnosed with a severe unknown viral infection. The condition lasted for a month.

By then I was learning that sickness is unpredictable, for it was two months later that I had the first signs of an intestinal disorder: a condition that would take months and months to cure.

At the advice of my primary doctor an appointment was made with a gastroenterologist who immediately recommended a colonoscopy. During that procedure a polyp was removed (the type that, if not discovered in its early stages, normally becomes malignant and can lead to colon cancer). Also tests revealed an irritation of the bowel caused by the radiation treatment for prostate cancer, resulting in constant intestinal cramps. Different medications were prescribed but the condition persisted for months. Then in October, I began to scratch what felt like a few mosquito bites. An office visit to my doctor confirmed my suspicions – shingles. I could not understand what had caused them. Shingles are usually associated with stress, and I did not feel stressed. I had no difficulty going to sleep. I slept seven to eight hours a night. I was able to meet all my financial obligations and I did not have any problems troubling me.

The doctor explained that there are two kinds of stress, emotional stress and physical stress which weakens the immune system making one susceptible to shingles. In a few weeks the shingles were gone.

Though a year had now passed since my first appointment with my gastroenterologist, I still needed his care. For some reason I began to bleed internally. So in February of 2001, I underwent several tests which revealed a bleeding ulcer. On January 27, 2002, after the fifth colonoscopy, the verdict was, "Healed ulcer."

Recalling all these events I remember what God brought me through. The goodness of the Lord was evident, and in all this, He was teaching me *"His ways are past finding out"* (Romans 11:33). He can and does use illness to accomplish His purposes. Did my surrender to the will of God include physical suffering? Was I willing to experience physical problems that I might be of greater service for Him? Could He break this body of mine and have me not ask, "Why?" but "What are you preparing me for?"

Along the Way

Along the Way

My Cross?

It is always difficult to set the record straight when loving, caring, well-meaning individuals make erroneous statements. Such was the case when on numerous occasions people referred to Jean as "my cross."

Never in twenty-two years of caring for her did I ever consider her as such. Never did I feel that she was a burden weighing me down or holding me back. Nor was she robbing me of the so-called pleasures of life. Had I not loved her, I could have become bitter against God as some do.

Without a doubt it was God who brought us together. Before a crowd of witnesses I had promised God that "in sickness and health" I would care for her. Long before each of us was born, God planned our physical make-up. He knew all about the genes we would inherit, those genes that would trigger ailments and diseases. As the omniscient God, He knew when we stood at that altar in Johnson City, New York, and were united in marriage all that Jean would experience in her life. Jean, His child, would need special care. By bringing our lives together, He trusted me to take care of one of His own. From the first day of her prolonged illness until the day He took her home, I always considered her a "trust." She needed someone to help her bathe, get dressed, get out of bed, get her meals, help her walk from one room to another, get in and out of a chair, wheelchair, or car, and I was God's choice to be that someone. Surely, if the Lord were in a physical body with the same limitations as Jean's, I would gladly care for my Savior, so as I would help Him, I helped Jean. That was my privilege. I am not the only one who has been given this privilege. In most congregations, there are people caring for a needy family member.

Of course it is not always possible to continue caring for a family member who needs constant supervision. On two occasions, separated by years, I inquired about the cost of placing Jean in a nursing home. I was completely exhausted. During the day I had outside help while I fulfilled my responsibilities, but at night I was getting little rest because of her physical condition. Though on medication, she had seizures during the night that kept me on constant guard. Thankfully, in answer to prayer, the seizures subsided and I was able to continue caring for her.

As a caretaker, I learned to be slow in saying what others should do and not do. Be slow to judge the motive for admitting a loved one to a nursing home. It may not be a lack of love, but a lack of stamina. Also, caregivers should be slow to say that they would never put one of their loved ones into a nursing home. They may have no choice.

God has not so constituted our bodies to relentlessly function for twenty-four hours a day over a long period of time. In a nursing home or similar facility, three groups of caregivers work eight-hour shifts. After work, many go home exhausted physically and emotionally. I thank the Lord for these special people who have dedicated their lives to care for a loved one when others were no longer able to do so.

Those who have had to admit a family member to a facility of special care need our love and understanding.

Sleep

One evening we were discussing as a family how long it takes to go to sleep. One of our grandsons remarked without any prompting, "As soon as grandpa goes to bed, he goes to sleep!"

Apparently, we are constantly being watched whether we realize it or not! By every action or reaction we are teaching. "Train a child in the way he should go."

A common behavior we often teach others is fear. Often the fear of something or someone is instilled in a child by the parent. However, when a child observes the unwavering faith of a parent, he is encouraged to trust God too, to see faith in action.

Our Lord's sense of safety was demonstrated to his disciples when they found him asleep in the height of a raging storm. (Mark 4:38). It took many years of spiritual growth before I could sleep during the storms of life. I, too, had sleepless nights worrying about some difficulty that was weighing heavily on my mind. All night long I struggled to come up with a solution to a problem but I could not. Then one day I realized a truth that I have passed along to many others with the hope that it might help. Though we all are made in the image of God, we are not like Him in all things. God has so made these bodies of ours that they need seven to eight hours of sleep a day. But God is Spirit. He never slumbers nor sleeps (Psalm 121:3, 4). Now since God is going to be awake, there is really no need for both of us to be awake all night! Therefore, I sleep believing that while I do, God is working. I lay my head on the pillow of the promises of God.

Now I must confess that there have been times when I have had to remind myself of this fact. At such times I find myself thinking, "You are in this bed for the sole purpose of getting some rest. Just relax and trust in His faithfulness."

A Small Church

Probably one of the most common questions asked about any church is, "How many attend?" I, too, have asked the same question. Usually the answer is either "a large church" or "a small church." Now it is not the number that troubles me, but importance given to that number.

When some hear of a large number in attendance at a service, they often conclude that God is truly blessing the work. They also surmise that the pastor must have a lot going for him since his ministry is attracting so many people. On the other hand, the pastor who is ministering to a small number must be limited in his capabilities. Yes, a pastor's ministry is often judged by the number attending the regular services. In fact, the tendency of many is to follow the large crowds and shun the small. After all, a packed car lot outside a church is very impressive, but does that determine whether or not God is blessing and approving what is transpiring inside?

Lately I have purposely been attending so-called small churches with the intent of encouraging those young to the ministry. And to my joy these young men are preaching messages that would be a help to all if aired on the television. I do not know of any of them who would not thrill at the privilege of ministering to hundreds or thousands. But what is more important to them? A large church building with hundreds attending or a ministry in the center of God's will?

One of my major concerns is the reason for parents choosing a church to attend. All too often the desirable church is the one equipped with the latest electronics equipment for teaching and a program of activities that appeal to their children. Now there may not be anything wrong with this approach, however, many parents are willing to sacrifice the preaching and teaching of the fundamental truths of God's Word for these advantages. Also, too many churches are allowing society to dictate the content of the message that flows from the pulpit. Consequently, today's children who are the church of tomorrow will be proclaiming a message less than Biblical.

Having said all this, is there such a thing as a small church? Can anything be classified as small when Jesus Christ, the Creator of the universe, is in the midst? How would you rate the following? A church service of 2,000 people without the presence of Christ, and a church service of twenty with His presence? How would God rate the two?

When the President of the United States meets with two or three leaders of other countries, it is described as a "big meeting." Is it not "big" because of the presence of the President?

Similarly, the presence of Jesus Christ in the midst of any number present makes the church "big." Jesus met one woman at the well (John 4:6-13). That meeting was so "big" it was recorded in His Word.

To that pastor who may regularly minister to twenty or so I say, Pray, prepare and preach as though you were being heard by 2,000. The Lord who is present hears you. It is not the number that counts but whether you are there in response to His leading and are faithfully and rightly dividing His Word. The pastor will never be asked when he stands before the Lord, "How many attended your church?"

Too Good to Suffer

We all know that both good and bad people suffer. Is there some common cause behind suffering? One such cause is revealed to mankind in the opening chapter of the Bible! The Fall of Man. Man's deliberate Fall into sin had sobering consequences, and suffering is one of them.

Some people even believe that an evil person deserves to suffer. But what some do have a problem with is why evil people do not suffer and good people do. It does not make sense. Should not the reward for being good be a trouble-free life?

One of my most troubling moments happened a few hours after I brought Jean home to New Bedford following her first operation in Boston. After I told our neighbor that the surgeon was able to remove only half of Jean's brain tumor, she said, "Jean is too good to suffer." I could not say, "You are right. She is too good to suffer." I certainly did not want to cast a cloud over Jean's life; that would not have been fair. Jean loved the Lord with her whole heart. Just as the Psalmist said in Psalm 42: 1, "As the heart panteth after the water brooks, so panteth my soul after thee, O God," Jean had a heart that panted for God.

For many days my spirit was troubled, so I prayed, "Lord, why is it that my spirit will not accept the thought that she (Jean) is too good to suffer?" The answer didn't come to me all at once, but over a period of time. It would be foolish for me to suggest that I know all the answers, but I do know that the good, perfect Son of God suffered. He suffered as a result of His full surrender to the will of His Father. In the Garden of Gethsemane did Christ's surrender result in immediate, rich blessing? No! In fact, Christ's surrender and subsequent suffering resulted in betrayal, humiliation, and pain.

John the Baptist is another example of one whose suffering fulfilled a specific purpose. His preparation of the people to receive Jesus (Isaiah 40:3) and his courageous exposure of sin cost him his head. John lived a hard life; eating locusts and wild honey and wearing camel's hair garments.

This man "too good to suffer" was decapitated (Mark 6:25-29). Surely it must have been a tremendous mental anguish to his disciples when they heard the news of his death. They must have cried out in agony, "Why, God, why? Why should evil people go free and this God-fearing, God-loving, good man die in this manner?"

Obedience to the will of God does not guarantee a life of blue skies. As to who may suffer and how and for what purpose, only God knows. However, there is one thing we can know: there is a purpose for every experience in life. God does nothing capriciously.

Many have a physical illness that seemingly does not fit into some master plan. Sometimes the Lord permits physical illness to show just who is in charge. It is so easy for us to believe that we can go it alone. God often finds it necessary to remind us that He is the giver and sustainer of life. The Bible alludes to this often: "Which of you by taking thought can add one cubit to his stature;" (Matthew 6:27). "For in Him we live and move and have our being" (Acts 17:28). "For without Me, ye can do nothing" (John 15:5).

Also, God sometimes chooses to stop us in our tracks so that He might, just like a parent, wrap His arms around us and show us His love. As our children got older and more independent, I often reached out and stopped them when they were running by me and said, "Give me a hug." or "Tell me what you are doing."

In other words, "Sit down so we can have a little talk together." "Little talks" with Jesus remove our anxiety and fear and when we grasp how much He loves us, peace and confidence flood our souls.

We may never understand the concept of suffering completely until we see our Lord in glory, but we can assuredly reiterate Paul's words in Romans 8: 28, "And we know that all things work together for good, to them that are called according to His purpose."

Leading the Way

Of al the lessons I've learned, one more must be added. The setting was the Adirondack Mountains of New York. For a number of years we took our boys camping at Golden Beach, Racquette Lake. It was there Jean had camped as a young girl with her parents and sisters. She knew how to set up a tent, operate a

Coleman stove fueled with white gas and a Coleman lantern and build a campfire.

For the first few camping vacations, she was the teacher and I was the student. Perhaps the only reason she did not chide me for being a slow learner was because I was her protection from the bears that frequently visited the campsites after dark. However, the one thing I never told her was that if a bear entered our tent she was on her own.

In the mountains we would hike to the fire tower. From the top of the tower platform we could see the top of mountains in two other states. The best time to be there was just before sunset. Hurrying with the evening meal and walking rapidly up the mile or more dirt road, we would arrive about ten minutes before sunset. Watching the sun set on the mountains reaching up to get the sun's last rays was unforgettable.

One time, however, we did not anticipate how fast darkness would fall. Before we were halfway back to the campsite, we were in total darkness. The children were far ahead of Mom and Dad. They were singing and having a good time. I knew we were safe because bears run away from manmade noise. As I listened to the boys singing chorus after chorus, I could not help laughing as I heard them sing, "My Lord knows the way through the wilderness. All I have to do is follow."

I remember an older woman in the New Bedford Church known to all as Grandma. Her life had been full of toil and sorrow. Her husband had died at a young age, leaving her with many children to care for, but her reliance was upon the Lord to give her strength.

In her eighties she asked me in a slow, deliberate manner, "Pastor, do all things *really* work together for good?" Then, having asked the question, she lifted her head heavenward as if to get her answer from above. After a brief pause, she turned back to me with a smile and said, "Oh yes, of course they do, of course they do."

Just as my children had led the way back to our campsite with their singing, this older saint had walked the way before me, modeling a godly life. May all of us who name the Name of Christ, especially those who are older in the faith, lead the way for those who follow. Jesus Christ is faithful and will always be there to help us along the way.

About The Author

Rev. Jim Tarr is a retired pastor who served congregations, the longest being in Pennsylvania at Paxinos Bible Church for 30 years. During much of that time, Jim cared for his invalid wife until she went to be with the Lord. Jim presently lives in Oldsmar, Florida, where he occasionally fills the pulpit for local churches. He also enjoys spending time with his grandchildren.

Printed in the United States
21842LVS00001B/52-69